DEATH AND NONEXISTENCE

DEATH AND NONEXISTENCE

PALLE YOURGRAU

OXFORD
UNIVERSITY PRESS

Oxford University Press is a department of the University of Oxford. It furthers the University's objective of excellence in research, scholarship, and education by publishing worldwide. Oxford is a registered trade mark of Oxford University Press in the UK and certain other countries.

Published in the United States of America by Oxford University Press
198 Madison Avenue, New York, NY 10016, United States of America.

© Oxford University Press 2019

CIP data is on file at the Library of Congress
ISBN 978–0–19–024747–8

9 8 7 6 5 4 3 2 1

Printed by Sheridan Books, Inc., United States of America

For Mary

CONTENTS

PREFACE

Buffalo Bill 's
defunct
            who used to
            ride a watersmooth-silver
                                stallion
and break one two three four five pigeons just like that
                                            Jesus

he was a handsome man
                        and what i want to know is
how do you like your blueeyed boy
Mister Death

—E.E. CUMMINGS[1]

The philosophy of death, now a domain of active research
in analytical philosophy, originated in recent years with

1. In his commentary on the poem, Thomas Dilworth (1995) writes that
"the speaker assumes it is better to be alive than dead. So death, which
cancelled Buffalo Bill's skill and erased his good looks, gives the speaker
an advantage over him. . . . Logically, the self-elevation of the speaker is
nonsense, since the dead (nonexistent) differ categorically from the living"

the publication of Thomas Nagel's seminal essay "Death."[2] Historically, Plato's dialogue *The Phaedo* is the locus classicus for philosophical discussion of death, while Parmenides's poem *Nature*—in particular, the first part, "The Way of Truth"—is no doubt where the philosophical debate about nonexistence, as such, began, taken up not long after by Plato in *The Sophist*. Among recent continental philosophers, Martin Heidegger's *Being and Time*, of course, is the urtext, followed not long afterward by Jean-Paul Sartre's *Being and Nothingness*. Two enormous books about nothing. "Nothing," or "the nothing," or "nothingness" is indeed an important subject discussed by Heidegger and Sartre, but it's not the focus of this book, though I will have something to say about nothing. Indeed, one of the primary theses of this study is that the dead, and more generally the nonexistent, are not nothing.

Though my approach differs radically from Heidegger's, my preoccupation, too, is with *die Seinsfrage*—the question of being (or Being). Like him—and unlike others in the analytical philosophy of death—I'm preoccupied with Parmenides and the question of nonexistence. Unlike him, however, I am an analytical philosopher who engages with modal logic, the

---

(174–75). It's not clear exactly what Dilworth means here by "differ categorically," but he appears to be suggesting that there's such a vast difference between the living and the dead that it makes no sense to compare them, and in particular, to suggest that the living enjoy an "advantage" over the dead. In any case, in this study, I will be arguing that the dead (the nonexistent) do not constitute a different category from the living. They can be compared, and the comparison reveals that the living do indeed have an "advantage" (albeit, a temporary one) over the dead. The "self-elevation" of the speaker is not "nonsense."

2. Nagel 1993.

semantics of proper names, and possible world theory. My philosophical roots are in Gottlob Frege and Saul Kripke, not Wilhelm Dilthey and Edmund Husserl.

In the background of this study are three essays I wrote about the philosophy of death in which, in contradistinction to others writing on this subject, I focused on the ancient problem of nonexistence. One can't do justice, I believe, to the metaphysics of death without rethinking fundamental questions of being. It's a mistake to think it suffices to merely reshuffle familiar concepts in clever ways. A new approach to metaphysics is needed, and I thought I had pointed out the direction that needs to be taken. In my innocence, I had hoped that no more needed to be said, but the reception of these essays—which have achieved, I think it's fair to say, some notoriety, if not acceptance—convinces me that much more needs to be said. I have therefore endeavored to set out the larger framework in which my approach finds its proper place.

In a sense, however, this goal is impossible to fully achieve, since the larger framework involves, among other things, providing an account of the nature of the existential quantifier, the semantics of proper names and indexicals, the ontology of fiction, the role of possible worlds as a foundation for quantified modal logic, the question of presentism in the philosophy of time in relation to the theory of relativity, modal set theory, and an analysis of what Parmenides, Plato, Aristotle, Aquinas, Kant, Russell, Frege, and Quine thought about the nature of existence, not to mention what contemporary philosophers like Saul Kripke, Ruth Barcan Marcus, David Kaplan, Nathan Salmon, and Timothy Williamson have written. Rather than attempting the impossible, an exhaustive, and exhausting, account of all these topics and thus delivering to the reader a massive tome—as seems more and more to be the custom these days—I've adopted a different approach. I've tried to delineate a clear path through this maze of difficult, fundamental philosophical issues, indicating where, and why, the path leads in a certain direction, choosing, only when it seems appropriate, to "stand and fight" for my ground, to persuade the reader of the soundness of my approach. My aim is thus, in Wittgenstein's sense, perspicuity, not the false hope of comprehensiveness.

Even this more modest goal, however, is made difficult by the fact that the themes I will be investigating are all closely related, so that I can't proceed in my argument in a simple, linear fashion. Musically speaking, my approach needs to resemble a Bach fugue rather than a Beethoven symphony. Since I'm not, however, composing a piece of music, I will, perforce, have to proceed otherwise. What follows, then, to change the image, will be a tapestry woven from a series of colored threads which criss-cross and touch each other throughout. A given theme will be taken up again and again, each time using a different colored thread to achieve an alternative perspective on the same problem, resulting, I hope, in a multicolored cloth containing a clear image of the logical landscape I seek to represent.

The book is written in the first person and, in general, is more personal in tone than my other writings, for a number of reasons. To mention just one, it was essential to respond in detail to some important reactions to my approach. To attempt to do this from a neutral, third-person point of view would have resulted only in stilted artificiality. The aim of my replies, however—which constitute only a small part of the book—is never merely polemical, but always designed to clarify, and thereby defend and contextualize, the new approach to the philosophy of death I'm proposing. Experience teaches me that often only when philosophers respond to their critics does one begin to understand what the philosophers were really saying.

I should add, finally, that this book, unlike most other recent philosophical studies in the field, is devoted primarily to the metaphysics of death, which has too often been neglected or taken to be too obvious to merit serious attention. Ethical, psychological, religious, and political questions are not my focus, though some of what I say here will have relevance outside the realm of metaphysics. Only in the final chapter do I turn my attention to questions beyond metaphysics.

I thank my colleague at Brandeis University, Berislav Marusic, who has, for a number of years, invited me to address his class about my work on the subject, and who has engaged me, after each lecture, in discussion of these ideas. Another Brandeis colleague, Eli Hirsch, made critical comments on an early draft of (what was then) the second chapter of the book, and corresponded with me about some issues relating to that chapter. I also corresponded with him and Thomas Scanlon at Harvard University about an issue concerning Derek Parfit. Jennifer Marusic, another colleague at Brandeis, offered helpful comments when I was composing a reply to a referee's report on the book proposal I submitted to Oxford University Press. Mary Sullivan, in addition to constructing the index, offered constructive comments on the text itself.

I thank Brandeis University for providing me with a one-semester sabbatical leave, and for granting me a one-semester

Senior Faculty Research Grant, to allow me time to work on the book. Finally, I thank my editor, Peter Ohlin, of Oxford University Press, for his support for the idea of the book and then for the book proposal itself, and for his patience in awaiting delivery of the final draft.

THE PARADOX

OF NONEXISTENCE

[I]f A were nothing, it could not be said not to be.
—BERTRAND RUSSELL

W. V. QUINE, IN "ON WHAT There Is,"[1] suggests that the answer to the question, "What is there?" is, obviously, "everything." After all, it would seem, there isn't, in addition to everything (*that is*), something that's been left out, which would have to be *what isn't*, since, there isn't, in addition to *what is, what isn't*. In case you're tempted, however, to bring *what is not* into the picture, Quine reminds us of an ancient puzzle, which he designates "the old Platonic riddle of nonbeing" or "Plato's beard," to wit: "Nonbeing must in some sense be, otherwise what is it that there is not?" For myself, this riddle, correctly understood, hides a deep truth, which I'll attempt to bring out in the following pages. Plato himself, of course, in *The Sophist*, wrestled with this paradox, which he took to be a deadly serious one (not simply, if you'll excuse the expression, a mere sophism). He acknowledged the father of the paradox, Parmenides of Elea, who famously declared, "It is not possible for 'nothing' [what is not] to

1. Quine 1961.

be."[2] Indeed, not only not to be, but not to have been or to be going to be, for "how could what is be going to be in the future? And how could it come to be? For if it came into being, it *is* not; nor *is* it, if it is at some time going to be. Thus becoming is extinguished and perishing is not to be heard of" (37–38). These grave pronouncements, which have darkened Western ontology ever since, came with a warning aimed at the realm of thought itself, for, as Parmenides also announced, "it is the same thing that can be thought and that can be" (31).

Now, I don't want, here, to take part in the scholarly dispute as to whether for Parmenides, "what is not" refers to predication (i.e. to what is not F, for some property F), or to facticity (i.e. to what is not the case), or to nonexistence. I will assume without argument, for the purpose of this discussion, that whatever else may be at issue in this ancient debate, existence is at least a central theme. My position is essentially that of Montgomery Furth in his classic article "Elements of Eleatic Ontology,"[3] where he argues that though Parmenides had what Furth calls a "fused notion of being" (fusing together the factive with the existential notions), faced with "the question whether this assimilation on Parmenides's part is of any importance in obtaining his conclusions . . . I shall propose . . . that the answer is roughly No" (247).

The force of the paradox of nonexistence has persisted over thousands of years, extending to Gottlob Frege's logic, in which there can be no truth-valuable statement in which

2. Cornford, F. M., transl. with an introduction, *Plato and Parmenides: Parmenides'* "Way of Truth" *and Plato's* "Parmenides" 1957, 31.

3. Furth 1974.

there is a singular term denoting what does not exist. For Frege, if any part of a sentence fails to denote (what exists), so does the entire sentence, the referent of which, if all the parts did refer, would be, according to Frege, a truth-value.[4] Given Frege's philosophy of language, that means that, just as Parmenides declared, one can't even think of what isn't. Paradox enters the picture due to the fact that it seems obvious, Parmenides notwithstanding, that there are plenty of things that don't exist—Aphrodite, for example (who is a mere myth), and the round square (which is impossible), as well as New York's World Trade Center towers (destroyed by terrorists), not to mention (more controversially) the past (no longer with us) and the future (not yet arrived). When you get right down to it, not only do some things fail to exist, *most things* do. And yet, if there are such things, such objects as the World Trade towers, "they" would have to be objects that don't exist, i.e. *nonexistent* objects—which sounds an awful lot like objects-such-that-there-are-no-such-objects— and we've fallen right back, it seems, into "the old Platonic riddle of nonbeing."

Bertrand Russell, with Frege a cocreator of modern logic, also took the riddle with deadly seriousness. In the spirit of Alexius Meinong, he argued in 1902 in *The Principles of*

---

4. Frege believed the referent of a sentence isn't a fact, which might seem the most natural view—assuming there is such a thing as the referent of a sentence. More recently W. V. Quine and Donald Davidson defended the view that there are no such things as facts. The argument against facts was formalized—but not defended—by Alonzo Church and Kurt Gödel. That allowed the argument to finally be refuted. See my essay "Frege on Truth and Reference" (Yourgrau 1987). I point out there where my approach differs from the similar one adopted by Jon Barwise and John Perry in "Semantic Innocence and Uncompromising Situations" (1981).

Mathematics[5] that the only way out was to introduce a third ontological category in addition to existence and nonexistence, which he called "being," declaring, *"Being* is that which belongs to every conceivable term, to every possible object of thought," whereas *"Existence,* on the contrary, is the prerogative of some only amongst beings" (449). Following directly in the footsteps of Parmenides, he declared that " 'A is not' must always be either false or meaningless. For if A were nothing, it could not be said not to be." "A is not," here, should not be taken as a denial of existence, but rather as a denial, so to speak, that "A is anything at all." As examples of beings that don't exist but are not "nothing at all," he mentions "[n]umbers, the Homeric gods, relations, chimeras and four-dimensional spaces."

As will emerge later, I believe Russell was onto something, but unfortunately, the details of his account, as put forward here, are replete with difficulties. To begin with, note what he says by way of explicating the concepts of being and existence, in particular, explaining how being differs from existence and nonexistence. Having pointed out that existence, unlike being, belongs only to some things, he says, about existence, "To exist is to have a specific relation to existence," which is, strictly speaking, to say nothing at all.

Why, then, introduce the distinction in the first place? "[T]his distinction is essential," he says, "if we are ever to deny the existence of anything. For what does not exist must be *something,* or it would be meaningless to deny its existence; and hence *we need the concept of being, as that which belongs even to the nonexistent"* (450; emphasis added). Here

---

5. Russell 1902.

he separates himself to some extent from Parmenides by attempting a solution to the paradox of nonexistence. He does not reject nonexistence, as such, but rather introduces a new ontological category, *being*. In effect, he accepts Parmenides's pronouncement, only interpreting "what is not" as indicating nonbeing rather than nonexistence. So far, so good. Indeed, in the following pages, I'll be arguing that what Russell is saying in these last few passages is absolutely right. The problems come later.

For Russell also accepts Parmenides's association of *what is* with *what can be thought*, thus, given his interpretation of what is as what has being, equating *being* with *what can be thought*.[6] Hence the generosity of his list of beings, which matches Meinong's. His philosophy of thought seems, like Meinong's, to directly mirror his philosophy of language, so that any meaningful singular term is taken to denote a genuine object, even if it is only, as it were, an object of thought. (Not for nothing does Meinong describe his account as *Gegenstandstheorie*, or theory of objects.) More, not only does Russell accept, with Meinong, that "the F" always refers, he appears also to agree with Meinong's principle that *the F is F*, or, a bit more formally, that *F(the F)*. This principle, however, unless somehow amended or modified, as he later realized, is logically disastrous.[7] It leads immediately to

6. Today, we distinguish belief, or thought, *de dicto* vs. *de re*, a distinction that would have to be taken into account in assessing Russell's neo-Parmenidean identification of what is with what can be thought.

7. Which is why neo-Meinongian logicians and philosophers do modify the principle, invoking a distinction between "nuclear" and "extranuclear" properties. This is not the place to assess how successful have been attempts to make out that distinction in a manner that is not ad hoc.

absurdities or outright contradictions, such as that the existent round square really is round and square and existent, and the nonexistent largest prime number really is both nonexistent and a prime number greater than every other prime number, etc.

Further, there are serious problems with Russell's list. At the time at which he was writing, 1902, the idea of a four-dimensional space seemed like a notion confined to the mathematical imagination, whereas today, thanks to Einstein, we take it to apply to the physical universe. As for numbers, for the mathematical Platonist or realist, like Russell's colleague Frege, numbers, as well as relations, are no less real than is the physical universe. Russell appears to be conflating, here, *the abstract* with *the nonexistent*, whereas the contrary of the abstract is, rather, *the concrete*. (We'll have much more to say about these contrasts later on.) Further, whereas it's a reasonable assumption that the singular term "the number three" refers to a particular object that figures prominently in the science of mathematics, nothing similar is true of the term "the round square," the paradigmatic use of which is probably such sentences as "There is no such thing as the round square."

The case of the Homeric gods, however, is trickier. The name "Aphrodite," for example, does seem, in some sense, to refer to a particular object, a particular Homeric god, and the name figures prominently in literary and historical contexts, such as Homer's *Iliad*, in which it's important not to confuse Aphrodite with, say, Athena. Indeed, as we'll see later, some contemporary philosophers, including Saul Kripke, believe that, at least outside fiction, the name succeeds in referring, albeit to an abstract construct of the imagination, while Nathan Salmon believes that the same is true even within fiction. Nevertheless, as Kripke insists—I think, correctly—there remains an important sense in which (unless one is a Greek polytheist) we need to remember that Aphrodite doesn't exist (or doesn't "really" exist), and what makes this true is not a fact that involves an ancient Greek goddess. What exactly does make this true, if not how things stand with Aphrodite, Kripke takes to be a genuine puzzle,[8] and here, too, I'm in agreement with him. By contrast, as I'll argue later, what makes true the nonexistence of Socrates is precisely how things stand with Socrates. As Nathan Salmon puts it in "What Is Existence?," " 'Napoleon exists' is false because of something to do with Napoleon" (2014, 250, note 8). Indeed, I take it to be a criterion of the incorrectness of a philosophy that it fails to distinguish the nonexistence of *Socrates* from the nonexistence of *Aphrodite*, i.e. fails to distinguish *the dead* from *the fictional*.

Russell's invocation, then, of a distinction between being and existence as a way of resolving the paradox of nonexistence is problematic, though it remains to be seen whether the essentials of his approach can be salvaged. It certainly appealed at one time to his friend and colleague G. E. Moore, and not only to him. Moore writes in "Being, Fact and Existence,"[9] "I used to hold very strongly, what many other people are also inclined to hold, that the words 'being' and 'existence' do stand for two entirely different properties . . . [that] many things which 'are' nevertheless do

8. See *Reference and Existence* (Kripke 2013, 155). Indeed, I agree with Kripke that it's not even clear that "Aphrodite doesn't exist" expresses a proposition. (Whom would this proposition be about?) See also Keith Donnellan, "Speaking of Nothing" (1974).

9. A lecture delivered winter 1910–11, reprinted in Moore 1978.

emphatically not exist. I did in fact actually hold this view when I began these lectures" (300). Indeed, it's been suggested that the distinction goes all the way back to the Stoics, and also to medievals like Duns Scotus.[10] However that may be, it was explicitly stated by Kant's older contemporary Christian Wolff. In *Being and Some Philosophers*,[11] Etienne Gilson quotes Wolff as saying: "Being is what can exist. . . . In other words, what is possible is a being . . . [Indeed,] possibility is the very root of existence, and this is why the possibles are commonly called beings . . . [W]e commonly speak of beings past and future, that is of beings that no longer exist or do not yet exist. . . . *Their being has nothing to do with actual existence*; it is though a merely possible being, yet a being" (114–15; emphasis added).

Wolff here goes considerably farther than Russell did in explicating the distinction, in particular, introducing the crucial idea of possibility. If we combine this with the view put forward by Kripke[12]—which I endorse—that fictional and mythological beings are not even possible, we're in a position to explain further why Aphrodite should not have been on Russell's list of beings, and to defend the distinction between Socrates and Aphrodite, between the dead and the mythological. (It should be clear enough why it's true to say

10. See Christopher Menzel 2014, "Supplement to *Actualism: Classical Possibilism and Lewisian Possibilism*," in the *Stanford Encyclopedia of Philosophy*. For a different view of the Stoics, see Nicholas Rescher, *Imagining Irreality: A Study of Unreal Possibilities* (2002, 117).

11. Gilson 1952.

12. *Naming and Necessity* (Kripke 1980, 158), reversing, as he points out, the position he incautiously took in "Semantical Considerations on Modal Logic" (Kripke 1971, 65), with regard to the possible existence of Sherlock Holmes.

that Socrates, though dead, is still possible, but in any case, I'll be going into this issue in considerable detail later.)

More recently, the distinction has been explicitly invoked in connection with possible-world approaches to the foundations of quantified modal logic (QML, henceforth), i.e. the logic of possibility and necessity that includes quantification over individuals. Christopher Menzel (2014), discussing in the *Stanford Encyclopedia of Philosophy* two prominent approaches to QML, possibilism and actualism, writes that "[c]lassical possibilism is rooted in the idea that there is a significant ontological distinction to be drawn between *being*, on the one hand, and *existence*, or *actuality*, on the other, . . . [b]eing . . . encompassing absolutely everything there is, in any sense. For the classical possibilist, every existing thing *is*, but not everything there is exists. Things that do not exist but could have are known as (*mere*) *possibilia*."

The distinction also appears explicitly in David Kaplan's "Afterthoughts,"[13] concerning his earlier work "Demonstratives,"[14] which he says was "dependent on the possibilist treatment of variables in the formal semantics" (579, note 29). He goes on to say, "I now incline to a form of language which preserves the distinction between what *is* (i.e. what the variables range over) and what *exists*" (579, note 29). No reference is made by Kaplan to Russell's invocation of the distinction, though Menzel does mention Russell, and in any case, it's clear enough that Kaplan's employment of it is a descendant of Russell's. Neither Menzel nor Kaplan,

13. Kaplan 1989b.

14. Kaplan 1989a.

however, refers back to the paradox of nonexistence, which clearly animated Russell. Alvin Plantinga's invocation of the distinction, however, in *The Nature of Necessity*,[15] does relate directly to that paradox.

Plantinga distinguishes what he calls the impredicative singular proposition, *It is false that Socrates has the property of existing*, from the predicative singular proposition, *Socrates has the property of nonexistence*, where a singular proposition[16] is taken to contain, in some sense, the object referred to by the subject term, not merely a conceptual representation of the object. The latter proposition, he says, "is true in no possible worlds whatever. If there *were* a world in which [the latter proposition] *is* true, then certainly in that world Socrates would *be* but not *exist*" (151; emphasis added). Though Plantinga rejects Russell's distinction between being and existence, I draw attention to this passage since it points to Plantinga's familiarity with it—and his assumption that his readers share this familiarity—and the condition he lays down (the truth of the latter proposition) that would constitute evidence for the correctness of the distinction.

---

15. Plantinga 1978.

16. The notion of a singular proposition originated, I believe, with David Kaplan, though ultimately, it goes back to Russell. See the (mutually frustrating) correspondence between Russell and Frege, reproduced in part in Nathan Salmon and Scott Soames (eds.), *Propositions and Attitudes* (1988, 56–57). "Mont Blanc," writes Frege, with exasperation, "with its snowfields is not itself a component part of the thought that Mont Blanc is more than 4,000 metres high" (56). What Frege says here may seem compelling, but as I point out in "Kripke's Frege" (Yourgrau 2012), when I think a Fregean thought – i.e. mentally engage with the thought, a constituent of Frege's "third realm" of abstract or Platonic objects – the thought itself is no more literally "in" the mind (whatever that might mean) than Mont Blanc, with its snow fields, is literally "in" the thought.

Interestingly, in a later essay, "On Existentialism,"[17] he reverses himself and maintains that there are worlds in which that proposition is true, without, however, recalling his previous position that this constitutes evidence for the soundness of the distinction between being and existence. It remains that Plantinga is clearly sensitive to the paradox of nonexistence, and to the role that the distinction between being and existence may, or may not, play in the resolution of that paradox.

Charles Parsons has also discussed the distinction in a section of his essay "Objects and Logic" entitled "Being and Existence,"[18] in which he recalls "the ancient question whether reference to objects is necessarily reference to objects that *exist*" (505). In his more recent study, *Mathematical Thought and Its Objects*,[19] he again has a section entitled "Being and Existence," based on his earlier essay, where he repeats a point he previously made, that "the distinction between being and existence is formally analogous to the distinction between existence and actuality that arose in our comparison between Kant and Frege" (24). He adds, however, that though "[i]t might be tempting to suppose that real existence is just Kant's and Frege's actuality and that what in mathematics is called existence is merely being[,] . . . [m]atters are not so simple" (24). We will discuss, in due course, the relationship between Kant's and Frege's ideas and the distinction between being and existence. For now, it's enough to point out that the distinction remains a lively source of debate among

17. Plantinga 2007.

18. Parsons 1982.

19. Parsons 2008.

contemporary philosophers and logicians. I would only add at this point that in contrast to Russell and Plantinga, Parsons does not appear to regard it, and thus what Meinong called a "theory of objects," as playing a decisive role in attempting to resolve the ancient paradox of nonexistence. On the contrary, according to Parsons, "discourse about *fiction* . . . is probably today the most plausible motivation for a theory of objects" (27; emphasis added).

I will be disputing, in due course, the contention that discourse about fiction is the most plausible motivation for a theory of objects, but Parsons is certainly right that as a matter of historical fact, contemporary theory of objects as practiced by neo-Meinongians has indeed tended to focus on fiction—and the question of fictional objects—as opposed to the paradox of nonexistence, in particular, the nonexistence of past and future objects. In the case of Parsons himself, it's worth noting that elsewhere in this section he says, "A straightforward semantics for modal quantificational logic involves a domain *D* of objects, which is independent of the choice of possible world. With respect to a given possible world *an object* in *D may or may not exist*" (24; emphasis added). One would have thought that a theory of objects, and thus the distinction between being and existence, would be highly relevant to the question of the role of objects—which "may or may or may not exist" with respect to a given possible world—in this account of the semantics of QML, yet, as we've just seen, Parsons suggests, rather, that the most plausible motivation for a theory of objects is discourse about fiction.

In sum, the paradox of nonexistence, "Plato's beard," which originated with Parmenides, has continued, explicitly or implicitly, to trouble philosophers, as has the distinction, in one form or another, between being and existence, which, at least since Russell, has been employed as a means to dissolve the paradox, and has acquired independent interest in a variety of contexts. If the paradox, and the distinction, have tended, nevertheless, to fade somewhat from prominence in recent discussions, the reason is no doubt due primarily to the fact that in 1905, Russell himself rejected his earlier 1902 stance in *The Principles of Mathematics*, abandoning not only his earlier adherence to the distinction, but Meinong himself, who has since become, in spite of a resurgence of neo-Meinongianism among some prominent logicians, a bête noire of analytical philosophy. The cry, appearances notwithstanding, "I'm not a Meinongian!"—reminiscent of earlier cries in a political context of "I'm not a communist!"—has been heard not a few times from a number of philosophers, including Parsons, Salmon, Timothy Williamson , and indeed, myself.

II

THE PREDICATE

OF EXISTENCE

"Being" is obviously not a real predicate.

—IMMANUEL KANT

IN 1905, IN HIS ESSAY "On Denoting," Russell reversed the position he had taken in 1902 in *The Principles of Mathematics* about the paradox of nonexistence, abandoning the distinction between being and existence and rejecting Meinong's principle that *F(the F)* on the grounds that it leads straightforwardly to contradiction. In what is now known as Russell's theory of descriptions, the paradox of nonexistence seems to disappear. Three crucial elements in this theory stand out. First, a sentence containing a definite description or "denoting phrase," "the F," such as "The F is G," is to be logically analyzed as "There exists a unique F, and it is G." More precisely, "There exists something, x, which is F, and anything that is F is identical to x, and x is G." In symbols: "$(\exists x)$ $(Fx \ \& \ (y)(Fy \supset y = x) \ \& \ Gx)$. Second, "ordinary" proper names, like "Aphrodite," are taken to be, in effect, disguised definite descriptions. So, for example, "Aphrodite" is to be analyzed as a ("disguised") definite description, "the A" (say, "the Greek goddess of love"). Third, existence is to be expressed only by the existential quantifier, "$\exists x$," and not by a predicate. The problematic sentence, then, "Aphrodite doesn't exist" is to be analyzed as "It's not the case that there exists a unique Greek goddess of love." In symbols, $\sim(\exists x)$ $(Ax \; \& \; (y)(Ay \supset y = x))$. In the final analysis, then, there is no singular term, no "denoting phrase,"[1] in Russell's terminology, in the fully analyzed proposition, hence nothing—no thing—for such a term to purport to refer to, which the sentence goes on to deny exists. No need, therefore, to introduce a distinction between being and existence.[2]

I've spoken of "ordinary" proper names. Russell contrasted them with what he called "logically proper names," terms attached to items with which we're directly acquainted in experience, as opposed to objects we can only reach via the conceptual apparatus provided by definite descriptions. Since a logically proper name A is meaningful only so long as

1. I'm simplifying here. The question of "the disappearance" of the denoting phrase in Russell's theory of descriptions is actually rather tricky. See David Kaplan, "What Is Russell's Theory of Descriptions?" (1970), and my essay "Russell and Kaplan on Denoting" (Yourgrau 1985).

2. It's worth pointing out that while Russell in 1905 was recommending what was in effect a deflationary, antimetaphysical approach to traditional philosophical questions, an approach that downplayed ontological imagination, Einstein in that same "miraculous year" of 1905 was exercising ontological imagination by introducing , with the assistance of Hermann Minkowski, four-dimensional Einstein-Minkowski space-time. The clash between to the two worldviews came to a head years later, when Russell visited Einstein, together with Kurt Gödel and Wolfgang Pauli, at the Institute for Advanced Study. "All three," wrote Russell, after the meeting, "were Jews [sic] and exiles, and, in intention, cosmopolitans, [who shared] a German bias for metaphysics." See my book, *A World without Time: The Forgotten Legacy of Gödel and Einstein* (Yourgrau 2005, 13). Ironically, both Russell and Einstein became, later, inspirations for the Vienna Circle of logical positivists. See Karl Sigmund, *Exact Thinking in Demented Times: The Vienna Circle and the Epic Quest for the Foundations of Science* (2017).

we're acquainted with its referent, its referent is guaranteed to exist as long as the name has meaning, and thus it can never be true to say, "A doesn't exist." So, once again, the paradox of nonexistence, attempting to refer to something only to deny its existence, seems to disappear.

Frege shared with Russell the idea that "ordinary" proper names have "cognitive significance" or conceptual content (which he called their "sense," a notion that Russell rejected in "On Denoting"), and also the idea that existence should be represented in a conceptually sound language (a *Begriffsschrift*, as Frege entitled the book that revolutionized modern logic) only via the existential quantifier. For both Frege and Russell, existence isn't a (first order) predicate or property of individuals, but rather, in effect, a (second order) property of concepts (or "propositional functions"), which may or may not have instances (otherwise put, under which objects may or may not fall). For Russell, "Saul Kripke exists" doesn't predicate existence of Saul Kripke, the individual. Rather, the sentence, misleading as it stands, should be reformulated as "The K exists," where "Saul Kripke" is taken to be short for a definite description "the K," and "The K exists," in turn, should be analyzed as "There is a unique x such that K(x)"; in symbols, "$(\exists x)(Kx \, \& \, (y)(Ky \supset y = x))$." For Saul Kripke to exist, according to this way of thinking, is for him to be the value of the variable "x"[3] which makes the sentence true. Hence Quine's famous slogan: To be is to be the value of a variable.

---

3. Strictly speaking, as Frege pointed out in correspondence with Russell, "x" isn't a variable, but rather a written sign, while to say "x is a variable" is to make an open statement, lacking truth-value. In the present context, I'll put such niceties aside.

Indeed, Quine, in "Existence and Quantification,"[4] is explicit in his agreement with Frege and Russell that "[e]xistence is what existential quantification expresses. . . . It is the existential quantifier that carries existential import" (94 & 97). Accepting Russell's theory of descriptions in broad outline, Quine, in "On What There Is," agreed with him that the old Platonic riddle of nonbeing had finally been resolved, and without, as Quine put it, "ruining the good old word 'exist'" (3) by introducing an imaginary distinction between what *is* and what *exists*—i.e. between *being* and *existence*. "We have been prone to say," wrote Quine, "in our common-sense usage of 'exist', that Pegasus doesn't exist, meaning simply that *there is no such entity at all*" (3; emphasis added).

However, P. F. Strawson, Quine's contemporary, was less enamored of "On Denoting." In "On Referring,"[5] he challenged the first element of Russell's theory of descriptions, as well as the doctrine of logically proper names. What's of special interest here, however, are the other two elements of Russell's theory. The so-called New Theory of Reference, spearheaded by Saul Kripke, Keith Donnellan, David Kaplan, et al., now widely accepted, challenged Russell's view that ("ordinary") proper names are simply disguised definite descriptions.[6] If this rejection of Russell's view is sound, as

4. Quine 1969.

5. Strawson 1950.

6. Strawson, in both "On Referring" and *Individuals* (1963), had already challenged Russell's view, denying that naming is the same thing as describing, although he insisted in *Individuals* that "[a] name is worthless without a backing of descriptions which can be produced on demand to explain its application" (7). He adds that "an 'identifying description' may, of course, include demonstrative elements . . . and may include a reference

I believe it is, it follows that there's no description available for substitution for a proper name in Russell's analysis, and

to another's reference to that particular" (185, note 1). A check is not the same thing as money in the bank, but at the same time, a check is worthless without money in the bank. "It is not merely a happy accident," Strawson wrote, "that we are often able, as speakers and hearers, to identify the particulars that enter our discourse" (3).

If Kripke, Donnellan, et al., were right, however, to insist that no such backing of identifying descriptions, including demonstratives, is essential to the proper use of proper names, is part of what linguistic competence consists in, it would be a mere happy accident—indeed, a kind of miracle—that when I ask at the counter for a plane ticket to London, the agent can correctly identify the referent of "London" and I end up flying to that city, since on Kripke's account, "It may even become the case that the great bulk, or *perhaps all* of what is believed to identify the object [referred to using a proper name], in fact fails to apply to it" (Kripke [2013], 13; emphasis added). It's a tenet of mine, however, that one should try to minimize the need for miracles in one's philosophy, and it would be a miracle indeed if the reason one ends up in London when one asks for a plane ticket to London is the fact that the Kripke-Donnellan historical name chain for "London" originated, unbeknownst to the ticket agent—or anyone else who uses the name—in London.

Donnellan himself, ironically, comes close to admitting his reliance on miracles. A miracle, let's assume, is an act performed by a divine being, an omniscient being, like God. Here, then, is how Donnellan characterizes his account of reference: "Suppose someone says, 'Socrates was snub-nosed,' and we ask to whom he is referring. The central idea is that this calls for a historical explanation . . . [concerning] an individual historically related to his use of the name 'Socrates'. . . . It might be that *an omniscient observer of history* would see an individual related to an author of dialogues . . . modeled upon that individual" ("Speaking of Nothing," Donnellan [2012], 96; emphasis added.) So, the reason why I get to London when I ask the agent for a ticket to London is because "an omniscient observer of history" can see that my use, and the agent's, of the name, "London," is historically related to London?

Clearly, there's something missing in Kripke's and Donnellan's account of proper names. If their theory, or "picture," of naming were the whole truth, it would be a mystery why proper names are of any *use*, a mystery *what the point would be* of using them.

thus the paradoxical negative existentials, such as "Socrates doesn't exist," that Russell struggled with in 1902, some of which seem clearly true, reappear. Indeed, the paradox has now been sharpened, given the doctrine of the New Theory of Reference that the thought expressed using a proper name will be a singular proposition (a conception we encountered earlier, discussing Plantinga), containing, in some sense, the referent itself, which would seem impossible if the negative existential is true and the referent doesn't exist.

The third element, too, of Russell's theory of descriptions, that existence isn't a first order predicate of individuals, has been not infrequently challenged. Already in 1963, in his seminal essay, "Semantical Considerations on Modal Logic,"[7] Kripke stated that, under certain conditions, "existence could . . . be defined in terms of identity, by stipulating that $E(x)$ means $(\exists y)(x = y)$" (70). He repeated his position in his John Locke Lectures of 1973, *Reference and Existence*:[8] "Now, in the Frege-Russellian apparatus of quantification theory itself there would seem to be a natural definition of saying that x exists: $E(x)$. Namely that there is a y which is x: $(\exists y)(y = x)$ (where x and y are both variables ranging over objects). So it is hard for me to see that they can consistently maintain that existence is only a second-level concept (in the Fregean terminology) and does not apply to individuals" (37). Kaplan has also taken Russell to task. "I do not understand," he wrote in "Afterthoughts" (1989), "why Russell did not recognize that the intolerable existence predicate could be defined by forming the indefinite description, 'an individual

---

7. Kripke 1971.

8. Now published as Kripke 2013.

identical with a', and then predicating existence of the indefinite description in the way Russell finds so commendable, '$(\exists x)(x = a)$'" (611, note 109).[9] Similarly, Salmon notes, in "Existence,"[10] that "the English world 'exists' may be defined by the phrase 'is identical with something', or more simply, 'is something'" (21).

So why did Frege and Russell fail to recognize what Kripke, Kaplan, and Salmon point out about the predicate of existence? "[T]he reason why Frege can get along without the predicate of existence," wrote Jaakko Hintikka in "Kant on Existence and Predication,"[11] "is that he assumes that all proper names (free singular terms) are nonempty" (259) (a fact I drew attention to earlier). "This is reflected," Hintikka continues, "by the validity of existential generalization in Frege's system: from any proposition F(b) . . . we can infer $(\exists x)(x = b)$. This obviously presupposes that b exists." And the same is true for Russell. In both of their systems, one cannot truthfully, indeed, even meaningfully, say, "Aphrodite doesn't exist" or "Socrates doesn't exist," assuming the New Theory of Reference is correct that proper names aren't disguised descriptions. If "Socrates" is not a disguised definite description, "$\sim(\exists x)(x = \text{Socrates})$" cannot be truthfully stated in either system.

9. He adds, it should be noted, that "[i]t is not my claim that the notion of *existence* is captured by the existential quantifier; variables can have any domain. My argument is *ex concessis*. Insofar as existence can be 'significantly asserted' of indefinite descriptions, it can be significantly asserted of names" (611, note 109).

10. Salmon 2008b.

11. Simo Knuuttila and Jaakko Hintikka, eds., *The Logic of Being: Historical Studies* (1986).

Surely, however, we do want to affirm the nonexistence of Aphrodite (though as Kripke has suggested, the matter is rather tricky), and I, for one (as I'll be arguing later), want to affirm the nonexistence of Socrates. Nor am I alone in affirming the latter. "Socrates's present nonexistence,"[12] says Salmon in "Nonexistence," does not "impugn the fact that 'Socrates' refers to him" (65). Which means that "Plato's beard," Parmenides's paradox of nonexistence, is still with us. So the question remains: *Who or what, exactly, is this Socrates, who isn't?* Do Kripke, Kaplan, Salmon, et al., of the New Theory of Reference, having, intentionally or not, given new life to this old paradox, have a new solution to it?

Salmon, in "Nonexistence," explicitly recognizes, in some sense, not only nonexistent objects, but what he calls impossible objects, objects that exist in no possible world, but, as far as I can tell, he says almost nothing about what this recognition consists in. The most I can find is a brief comment confined to a footnote, where he says, concerning impossible objects, that "it is difficult to deny that in *some* sense, there are such objects to be quantified over. . . . A *substitutional* interpretation of 'there are' may be called for when impossible objects raise their ugly heads" (62, note 24; emphasis added). Whatever one makes of the notion of substitutional quantification, however, it seems a bit perverse to ask us to recognize as genuine *objects* entities whose ontological status can be recognized not by *objectual* quantification but only by

12. I'm disconcerted by Salmon's speaking of Socrates's *present* nonexistence, instead of simply speaking of his nonexistence, though I'm glad to see that at one point, he does speak of someone's " conced[ing] that Socrates does not exist" (66). If asked by a student if Socrates is alive, I would hardly reply, "Not presently."

substitutional quantification—according to which *(∃x)(Fx)* is true iff there is a *name* that, substituted for the variable, *x*, makes *Fx* true, as opposed to objectual quantification, where there needs to an *object* in the domain that, taken as a value of *x*, makes *Fx* true.

How about nonexistents that aren't impossible, which Salmon also in some sense recognizes? What he says about the ontological status of these is confusing. In "Existence," he says that "[by] contrast with Meinongians, I am not claiming that there are individuals that do not exist. . . . What I am claiming is that there *might have* been individuals that do not actually exist" (43). Yet in "What is Existence?" he says that "['*a* exists'] is false exactly when the designation of *a* is something that does not exist. . . . The existential quantifier [I am employing] is not restricted to individuals that exist. It includes non-existent individuals" (246). Here, then, he says explicitly that he is existentially quantifying over non-existent objects, where the quantifier, obviously, doesn't represent (actual) existence. So what exactly *does* it represent? Mere possible existence? Is he saying only that there *possibly exist* individuals that don't actually exist (which actualists will have no trouble accepting), or that in some sense there *exist* individuals that are merely possible and don't actually exist (which sounds like Meinongianism, which Salmon says he rejects)? If the latter, what exactly is the sense of "exist" he has in mind?

Kripke I find also to be curiously difficult to pin down on the ontological status of possible individuals. In "Semantical Considerations on Modal Logic," his semantics includes a set, K, described as "the set of all 'possible worlds'" (64), and for each H that is a member of K, there is assigned a domain consisting of "the set of individuals existing in H"

(65). "Intuitively," he writes, "in worlds other than the real one, some actually existing individuals may be absent, while new individuals, like Pegasus, may appear. . . . Holmes does not exist, but in other state of affairs, he would have existed" (65). In spite of his apparent quantification over or reference to possible people, would Kripke say, as Salmon did in "Existence," "I am not claiming there are individuals that do not exist. . . . What I am claiming is that there *might have been* individuals that do not actually exist"? (43).

From some remarks in his much later preface to *Naming and Necessity* concerning possible worlds (to be discussed later), it would seem that Kripke shares Salmon's position. Compare, however, the way Ruth Barcan Marcus, in "Possibilia and Possible Worlds," understands Kripke. "In allowing domains of possible worlds," she writes, "to include nonactual individuals, Kripke allows for possibilia. . . . The semantics for Kripke's theory appear to be symmetric between referring to actual objects and referring to possible objects. . . . No special problem is noted about assigning possible objects to individual variables serving as individual constants" (1993, 205–6). All this Marcus herself rejects. "Actual objects," she says, "are there to be referred to. Possibilia are not. . . . A possible object is not there to be assigned a name" (205). I'm unhappy with Marcus's critique of Kripke, in particular, with her remark that merely possible objects are not "there" to be assigned a name, and will discuss her views in due course, but I agree with her characterization of what Kripke appears to be doing in his seminal essay, as opposed to the way he expressed himself in his later preface.

In any case, here's what I think. Quine's bon mot, "Nonbeing must in some sense be, otherwise what is it that there is not?" correctly understood, represents a deep truth.

The key is to read "nonbeing," here, as standing for *nonexistence* and to take "be" to represent *being*. The deep truth, then, is **the nonexistent must *be*, otherwise what is it that fails to *exist*?** Quine's statement that "we have been prone to say, in our common-sense usage of 'exist', that Pegasus doesn't exist, meaning simply that *there is no such entity at all*," is true of a fictional "entity" like Pegasus,[13] but not of a historical

13. Given that there is no such entity as Sherlock Holmes, no such being, it follows that, just as Parmenides stated, we cannot so much as *think* of (in a *de re* sense) or refer to "it," not even to deny its existence. The *nonexistent* may *be*, as I've been arguing—they have some ontological status— but Parmenides is right that *nonbeing*, as such, does not in any sense be. So to speak, there's no something at all about nothing. But then, "What can someone mean," as Kripke says, "when he says that Sherlock Holmes does not exist? Is he talking of a definite thing and saying of it that it does not exist?" (*Reference and Existence*, 144). Of course not. Then what does one mean by such a statement? Kripke proceeds to shoot down what appear to be all the plausible interpretations, including the most obvious one, that one is really referring to the name "Sherlock Holmes" and denying it a referent.

"I am very suspicious," he also says, "of a view that takes the denial of existence to mean 'fictional' or 'not real'" (149). He thus rejects the kind of approach that has become quite popular these days, a good example of which is presented by Tatjana von Solodkov in "Fictional Realism and Negative Existentials" (2014). "My proposal," she says, "borrows an idea from Thomasson in that it involves the claim that negative existentials may be interpreted by reference to particular kinds. Hence, 'Hermione doesn't exist' will be true in a context iff Hermione is not a K_c. The value of K in a given context [c] will be typically fixed to a semantic value that may be chosen from a range of appropriate values, most prominently *concrete object* and *serious object*" (351). Having rejected such views, Kripke confesses that "I have a certain tendency at this point to throw up my hands. . . . It does seem to me to be a genuine and unsolved problem—perhaps the most difficult in the area" (155).

Indeed, the problems concerning empty names are so difficult that a proposal he puts forward seems to conflict with a tenet of his own account of "direct reference", according to which proper names are not associated with intensional entities like Fregean "senses." He suggests that "[I]n

entity like Socrates. To say that Socrates is dead, hence non-existent, is not to say that *there is no such entity as Socrates.* "Socrates does not exist" is true in virtue of how things stand with *Socrates,* whereas Pegasus's nonexistence is not the case because of how things stand with Pegasus. When *Time* magazine announced the death of bin Laden, it put a picture of him on the cover with a big X across it indicating that he had been "crossed out," eliminated from existence. *Time* had it right. In spite of his death, his nonexistence, there is such a person as bin Laden. Imagine if an editor of *Time*, a student of Quine's, had rejected the idea of this cover, since, as Quine would have it, bin Laden doesn't exist,[14] so there is no such person as bin Laden to be represented. The truth, however, is that bin Laden's nonexistence is only possible in virtue of the fact that *there is* such a person as bin Laden who fails to exist. Something cannot become nothing, just as nothing cannot become something. *Ex nihilo, nihil fit.*

I disagree, therefore, with Peter van Inwagen, who says in *Existence: Essays in Ontology* that "[m]any philosophers distinguish between being and existence. . . . Following Quine,

---

the sentence 'The astronomer believes that there is a proposition about Vulcan, saying of Vulcan that it is red', the phrase 'about Vulcan' is a special sort of quasi-intensional use" (156). Salmon calls attention, dramatically, to this conflict: "The account [put forward by Kripke] ultimately involves an intensional apparatus. Indeed, it appears to involve *industrial strength intensional machinery* of a sort that is spurned by direct-reference theory" ("Nonexistence," 74; emphasis added).

14. In point of fact, as we'll see later, Quine wouldn't have agreed that bin Laden doesn't exist, since he was a spatializer of time, a classic four-dimensionalist, who believed that past, present, and future events or objects all exist equally (though not all at the same "locations" in space-time). He would still have acquiesced, however, to the conditional: if bin Laden doesn't exist, there is no such entity at all.

I deny there is any substance to the distinction. . . . To say of a particular individual that it exists is to say that *there is such a thing*" (2014, 58 & 59; emphasis added). Historians continue to be fascinated by Napoleon, though he's been a long time dead. Would van Inwagen not agree that *there is* such a person as Napoleon, even though Napoleon has long ceased to *exist*?

Though van Inwagen rejects my approach, it should be taken seriously by Kaplan,[15] Kripke, and Salmon, who have insisted that existence is, or can be, a predicate of individuals. As William Kneale, in 1936, affirmed in "Is Existence a Predicate?," "The fundamental thesis of those who believe existence to be a predicate [of individuals] is that there is a sense of 'being' logically prior to existence." I endorse that fundamental thesis. As I said earlier, Russell in 1902, in distinguishing being from existence, was onto something, though he hadn't thought it through sufficiently. His theory of descriptions, whatever its merits as an account of definite descriptions,[16] served only to sweep under the rug the problem of nonexistence. Quine, in "On What There Is," succeeded only in wielding Russell's broom.

So what exactly is *being*? Well, what exactly is *existence*? Being, I suggest, should be taken as a primitive notion represented formally by the existential quantifier—informally by the words "there is"—and the predicate of existence should also be taken as primitive, in particular, not as

---

15. As we'll see later, Kaplan actually comes very close to acknowledging the distinction between being and existence (between "is" and "exists").

16. See the special issue of *Mind*, 2005, honoring the one hundredth anniversary of the publication of "On Denoting," especially Kaplan, "Reading 'On Denoting' on Its Centenary," and Kripke, "Russell's Notion of Scope."

definable in terms of identity and existential quantification. But although being can no more be defined than can existence, one can nevertheless say more about it than Russell did. Elucidation is not confined to definition. As I view it, being is an ontological category that is a bridge between existence and nonexistence, underlying both. It's not a form of *existence*, not even in Timothy Williamson's special "logical sense of existence," which will be discussed later. I reject therefore José Benardete's claim in "Nonexistent Entities," in *Metaphysics: The Logical Approach*, that "we can only relish the opportunity to regress to an ulterior substratum of reality that underlies even existence itself. But no such stratum or substratum is likely to be found" (1989, 69). Unlike existence and nonexistence, *being* does not wax and wane, just like *possibility*, which suggests an intimate relationship between the two. (Recall Menzel's comments about "possibilism" as a foundation for QML.) Whether that relationship is identity I leave open.[17] I'm not claiming, as Salmon did in "Existence," only that "there *might have been* individuals that do not actually exist." I'm claiming that there *are* individuals that do not actually exist. Before he actually existed, Socrates was one of those individuals. It's not just that before Socrates existed, there *might have been* such a person as Socrates who could, in the course of time, come to exist, but rather that before he existed, there already *was* such a person as Socrates. He couldn't have become actual if he wasn't already possible, and

---

17. Salmon, as we saw previously, in recognizing, in some sense, impossible objects, would appear to reject, in effect, the idea that the relationship between possibility and being is identity, although, since he doesn't explicitly introduce the notion , it's difficult to attribute to him a thesis about the nature of being.

he couldn't have been possible if there wasn't already such a person as Socrates.

All of which begs the question: What beings are there? And how do we discover them? There is no pat answer. Why should there be? Is there a pat answer as to what *existents* there are? Was there a pat answer to the question of whether the Higgs boson existed? Is it a trivial matter to find out if the names "Homer" and "Moses" refer to genuine beings (now nonexistent), or if their origins are based on fiction? Is it easy to determine if the name "God" refers to something existent? I've already taken exception to Russell's 1902 partial list, which took the path of least resistance. *Pace* Russell and Meinong, there is no semantic algorithm for determining which singular terms denote genuine beings (existent or nonexistent)— for determining which terms succeed in *referring*—any more than there is an algorithm for determining which sentences are *true*. *Semantic naiveté*—the Meinongian-Russellian view that all singular terms, as such, succeed in referring, and referring to what they denote or describe[18]—is no substitute for serious ontological investigation. We know, for example, that "Socrates," though the name fails (at least on my view) to refer to an *existent* being, nevertheless refers to a (nonexistent) being. Since at one time

---

18. The additional characterization is important. Frege, at one point, determined to ensure that all singular terms in his formalization of logic have a referent (that exists), suggested, in effect, that one simply "legislate" that if a term, conventionally understood, lacks a referent, henceforth, the referent will be taken to be the null set, which in Frege's "set theory" (as in contemporary set theory), cannot fail to exist. Exactly what could be gained by such an artificial device is a good question. The irony seems to have been lost on Frege that the null set, which is as close to *nothing* as anything can get, is to be taken as a guarantor that every term refers to *something*.

this being actually existed, we know that *there is* something the name refers to. Having a referent should not be confused with having an *existent* referent, just as being an object should not be confused with being an existent object.

Though he's an object, Socrates is a nonexistent object. By contrast, "Sherlock Holmes," on the theory of fiction I espouse, is a name used in fiction *to pretend to refer* to a real detective, not a name used *to refer* to a pretend detective, which is why Kripke was right to reverse what he wrote earlier about Sherlock Holmes and affirm that Sherlock Holmes is in addition to not being actual, not even possible. If there's no one you're referring to, ipso facto, there's no one you're referring to who's *possible*. This remains true, outside fiction. When scientists denied the existence of phlogiston, they could not, reasonably, have insisted, nevertheless, on its possibility, since, if their account was correct, there was no "it" there to be so much as possible.[19]

---

19. Following Kripke's discussion in *Naming and Necessity* of mental/physical identity theories and his example concerning the identification of pain with c-fiber firings, we must distinguish the supposed possible existence of phlogiston from the genuine possibility that there might have been something else responsible for the effects phlogiston was postulated to explain than what in fact we take to be responsible. There are possible worlds where something other than what's actually responsible for these effects is responsible for them, but it won't be *phlogiston* that's responsible in those worlds.

Strictly speaking, however, since "phlogiston" in fact fails to refer, my remarks here, in order to have a truth-value, should be paraphrased so as to avoid using this name. Exactly how to do so is a nontrivial matter. Kripke himself, in *Reference and Existence*, fell into a trap here. After noting that "on my view, if statements containing 'Sherlock Holmes' express pretended propositions—or, rather, pretend to express propositions—one can't speak of a pretended proposition as possible" (40), he goes on to say, concerning what he elsewhere called epistemic possibility: "If it turns out that Sherlock Holmes really exists, then my supposition that the name is fictional is

Symbolically, the nonexistence of Socrates should be represented as ~E(**Socrates**), from which it follows by existential generalization that (∃x)(~Ex) (i.e. there is something that doesn't exist), and more specifically, that this something is Socrates, i.e. that (∃x)(x = **Socrates** & ~Ex).[20] I disagree, then, with Kripke, when he says in *Reference and Existence*, "I agree with Russell that it couldn't have been the case that 'something' didn't exist" (37). Socrates is something, and he doesn't exist.[21] He is a nonexistent something, *a nonexistent object*, but he is not, therefore, an-object-such-that-there-is-no-such-object. Rather, he is an-object-such-that-there-*exists*-no-such-object.

I agree with Kripke, however, when he says in *Reference and Existence*, "Things are not of two kinds, existers and nonexisters" (37) (though he meant something different by this than I do). Existers and nonexisters are not two separate *kinds* or *species* of beings, as Kant recognized. Nevertheless,

wrong" (41). If, however, as he believes, the name is in fact fictional, it follows that his last statement fails to express a proposition. (Ironically, assuming that Barack Obama exists, the sentence, "If it turns out that Barack Obama doesn't really exist, the supposition that his name is not fictional is wrong," though bizarre, does express a proposition.)

20. Note that the same analysis can't be applied to statements about the nonexistence of fictional or mythical characters like Santa Claus. It's not true that (∃x)(x = Santa Claus & ~Ex), nor that ~(∃x)(x = Santa Claus & ~Ex), since, by hypothesis, "Santa Claus" fails to refer, and thus both statements lack truth-value. Exactly how to correctly express the nonexistence of Santa Claus is a fraught issue. No wonder Kripke in *Reference and Existence* said, as noted above, that he had a tendency "at this point to throw up my hands.... It does seem to me to be a genuine and unresolved problem . . . ."

21. If what Kripke meant by "something" was "something that exists," what he said was true, but trivial . Indeed, not infrequently in such discussions, it's not made clear what exactly is meant by "something."

existing and not existing are two different *states of being* that a single entity, like Socrates, can occupy at different times, just as one and the same being can in one possible world be actual, and in another, merely possible,[22] *the possible and the actual also not being two separate kinds or species of being*, but rather two different *modes of being*.

Still, it's not clear in what sense existence can be a predicate of individuals, since, as Kant pointed out, it seems to add nothing to the description of an individual to say that it exists. Thus, as Kripke notes in *Reference and Existence* (35, note 6), "Many have connected Russell's analysis with the Kantian doctrine that existence is not a predicate." As Kripke sees it, however, Kant's position "doesn't seem to me, as far as I am able to read him, to be identifiable with that of Frege and Russell" (35, note 6). Kripke points out that what Kant actually said was only that existence is not a "real" predicate, but only a "logical" one: "[According to Kant,] when we deny existence of a subject, we don't deny a predicate of it, but rather reject the subject together with all its predicates. . . . [Similarly,] saying of an object that it exists is different from ascribing a property to it, in the ordinary sense of 'property'" (35–36, note 6). I agree both with what Kripke says here about Kant and with what Kant himself is saying. If I ask Jascha Heifetz to describe his violin and he says it's old, Italian, made by Stradivarius, dark brown in color, etc., it would be absurd for him to come back later to tell me that he had inadvertently left out a crucial property in his description, namely, existence (adding, perhaps, that that's what makes it so expensive)!

22. If one believes, as I do, along with Kripke and many others, in transworld identity.

Salmon, curiously, in "What is Existence?," says, "I subscribe to the *existence-as-predicate theory*, which Kant and his followers reject and *which Kripke dismisses*" (251; emphasis added). In *Reference and Existence*, Kripke says explicitly that "my view is that it is perfectly legitimate to attribute existence to individuals" (36). Salmon is right, however, to say that Kripke "is sympathetic to the spirit of the metaphysical Kantian thesis" (249). He draws attention to Kripke's statements in *Reference and Existence* that "you are not attributing a property to Napoleon when you say he exists—you are saying there is such a thing for properties to be attributed to. That in some obscure sense seems to me to be true, and it is perhaps what Kant had in mind" (146). Salmon agrees that Kant may have had this in mind, but takes exception to Kripke's sympathy for Kant: "[T]he 'rather obscure' observation seems to me to be simply false. . . . What is this—*being a candidate for having a property*— . . . but a special property of x . . . ?" (250). Salmon appears to have forgotten something else Kripke said about Kant, which I alluded to above, namely, that Kant's doctrine is that "saying of an object that it exists is different from ascribing a property to it, *in the ordinary sense of 'property'*." That was my point, above, about the properties Heifetz might ascribe to his violin, "in the ordinary sense of property." Kripke, like Kant, isn't denying that there is another sense of "property," namely what Kant calls the "logical" sense. Employing the property of existence in this sense, Heifetz can ascribe it to his violin.

Salmon appears to have a kind of blind spot when it comes to Kant's approach to this subject. He beats Kant over the head again and again for going on to say, after pointing out that "[b]eing' [i.e. existence] is obviously not a real predicate; that is, it is not a concept of something which could be added to the concept of a thing," that "*the real contains no more than the merely possible.* A hundred real [dollars] do not contain the least coin more than a hundred possible [dollars]."[23] On the contrary, says Salmon in "What Is Existence?": "It is simply and flatly wrong that a real dollar is not worth one cent more than a merely possible dollar. If one merely possible dollar is subtracted from one real dollar, the remaining amount is exactly $1. . . . A hundred existent dollars has greater monetary value than a hundred *merely possible* dollars" (249). And again, in "Existence": "I find it impossible to agree with [Kant], however, that a hundred existent dollars is not worth one penny more than a hundred merely possible dollars. If all my dollar bills were merely possible, I would gladly trade them for just one existent dollar bill" (24).

Salmon acts as if Kant might try to impress you by padding his bank account by including merely possible dollars, whereas Kant, not being a lunatic, says explicitly, "My financial position is, however, affected very differently by a hundred real [dollars] than it is by the mere concept of them (that is, of their possibility)" (A599; B627). Salmon takes this remark to reflect a moment of sound sense from Kant, followed, however, by what he calls "a giant leap backward," Kant's remark that "the conceived hundred dollars are not themselves in the least increased through acquiring existence outside my concept." What Kant is saying, however, is that the *content* of a concept is not in the least changed when the

---

23. *The Critique of Pure Reason* (A599; B627; emphasis added) (Kant 1965).

concept is realized. If I'm dreaming of finding one hundred dollars and then my dream comes true, it's only *my actual dream*, so to speak, that came true, if what I find is exactly one hundred dollars, not, say, two hundred dollars, i.e. if the *actual content* of the concept entertained in my dream was realized. My dream hasn't come true if *what was realized* isn't exactly *what was in my dream*. That was Kant's point. If Salmon were right, life would be sad indeed. Our dreams would never come true. Your daughter's dream of owning a white pony would never be realized, for the white pony you give her would be a *real* pony, something that according to Salmon is entirely different from a *dream* pony, the pony of her dreams. When your daughter dreamed of owning a white pony, however, what she dreamed of was owning a real pony, not a dream pony.

What Kant meant by saying that "the real contains no more than the merely possible" is that the real and the possible are not two different *kinds* of things, two different *species* of objects. What separates the real from the merely possible, the existent from the nonexistent, he's saying, correctly, is not their *nature* or *essence* (what Kant calls "the concept" of them), but only their *existence*. (Recall my earlier comments about Kripke's claim that "[t]hings are not of two kinds, existers and nonexisters.") What distinguishes the actual from the possible, the existent from the nonexistent, is not *what* they are, but *whether* they are. When Salmon compares a hundred real dollars with a hundred possible dollars and declares the real to be much more valuable, saying that if all his dollars were merely possible, he'd gladly trade them in for just one real dollar, he's talking as if real dollars and possible dollars are *two different kinds of thing*, one more valuable than the other, whereas Kant, correctly, insists that the real and the possible are precisely *not* two different kinds of thing. The reason one prefers real dollars to possible dollars is not based on *what* the two are, but rather on *whether* they are, not their nature, but their existence.

Salmon, however, is not alone in misreading Kant and thus missing the importance of what Kant is saying. Hidé Ishiguro, in "Possibility," also objects to Kant's famous dictum. "We should remind ourselves," she writes, "of the wise remark of Brentano . . . [that] 'the truth is that a hundred imaginary dollars is not just one, but a full hundred dollars less than a hundred [real] dollars.' . . . As Brentano says, possible dollars are not sums of dollars at all. They are not a *kind* of dollar—as a 1979 Hong Kong dollar or an 1800 US dollar would be. Similarly, a possible world is not a *kind* of world like a chaotic world or a far-away world. It is an object of thought which could have been realized as a world, but was not" (1980, 86; emphases added). Ishiguro here gets Kant exactly backward. As I've been emphasizing, it was precisely *Kant's* point that possible dollars *aren't* a kind of dollar! Ishiguro, perversely, accuses Kant of a thesis he is at pains to deny.

As to Ishiguro's final comments about the relevance of Kant's dictum to the question of possible worlds, I'll confine myself for now to the following remarks. What exactly does Ishiguro mean here by calling possible worlds "objects of thought"? The clue is to be found earlier in her essay, where she writes that "[p]ossible worlds, then, *are not worlds* which I think about . . . but are, I suggest, abstract entities . . . whose existence is invoked in my modal theories as *models of my imaginative thoughts. . . .* [P]ossible worlds and possible objects are *constructs of thought*, they are not the kind of things to which actual things and the actual world can stand in any relation" (79 & 85; emphases added). I daresay that Ishiguro is not alone in seeing things this way. I believe, however, that this is a consequence of her missing the force of Kant's famous dictum, from which it follows, contra Ishiguro, that possible worlds and possible objects (including possible people) are not *different kinds of things* from you and me and the actual world, are no more mere "constructs of thought" than are you and I and the actual world. It would, indeed, be a miracle if a mere *construct of thought* "could have been realized as *a world*," if a mere construct of thought could have been "realized" as your daughter.

Kit Fine makes a similar point in "The Problem of Possibilia": "Suppose . . . that it is maintained that every (merely) possible person is identical to an actual property—one perhaps that specifies its 'essence'. Consider now a possible person. Then it is possibly a person. But no property is possibly a person and so no possible person is identical to a property: for there is a possibility for the one, namely that of being a person, which is not a possibility for the other" (2005, 216). I would put this, however, a bit differently from the way Fine does. It's not that a possible person has the *possibility* of being a person. A possible person *is already* a person, who, unlike a property, has the possibility of becoming (an) *actual* (person). That was Kant's point when he said that the real contains no more than the merely possible. As I pointed out earlier, modality represents not two different *kinds* of being, but rather two different *modes* of being, being possible vs. being actual. The *kind* of being at issue here is being a *person*. A person can possibly exist or can actually exist. In the former case, we speak of a possible person, in the latter, an actual person, a form of speech that can give the false impression that we are referring to two different kinds of beings, possible persons vs. actual persons. Kant saw through this illusion, but clearly, it's been difficult for some philosophers to see what Kant saw.

III

NONEXISTENCE

AND DEATH

For living things, it is living that is existing.

—ARISTOTLE

IF OUR REASONING HAS BEEN along the right lines, we can proceed on the assumption that there is no obstacle to taking the predicate of existence to apply to individuals, though, as our discussion of Kant has brought out, we need to be clear about what exactly it means to apply what Kant calls a merely "logical" predicate like existence. We can take "Socrates doesn't exist," then, Russell and Quine notwithstanding, to express just what it appears to, namely, the fact that the individual, Socrates, doesn't exist, that he lacks the property of existence or has the property of nonexistence. But is it in fact true that Socrates doesn't exist, as I've been assuming, without argument? My assumption was based on the uncontroversial fact that Socrates is dead, and that as Aristotle said, "for living things, it is living that is existing."[1] If, for Socrates, living is existing, not living—being dead—means not existing. This assumes, of course, that Socrates is "a living thing," which seems, however, to be contradicted by the fact

---

1. Aristotle, *De Anima*, Bk II, Ch. 4, 415b.

that *this living thing is dead*, hence, *not living*! Was Aristotle, who invented logic, committing a simple logical blunder?

Of course not. By "a living thing" Aristotle indicated something's essence. But one should distinguish two senses of essence. Essence* constitutes those properties something simply cannot lose. Essence** constitutes those properties something cannot lose while continuing to exist.[2] Part of Socrates's essence* is to be a living-thing, a thing which cannot exist unless it's alive. Part of Socrates's essence** is to be alive. Socrates is dead. He is a living-thing that has ceased to be alive, which is why he has ceased to exist. A living-thing is an organic thing, like a plant or an animal, as opposed to an inorganic thing, like a rock or a snowflake. When a living thing dies, it becomes a *nonexistent living-thing*. It does not become *an inorganic thing*. When you die, you don't turn into a rock or a snowflake. You forfeit your existence, not your essence*.

But was Aristotle right in assuming that life is essential to living things? Fred Feldman thinks not. In *Confrontations with the Reaper: A Philosophical Study of the Nature and Value of Death*, he rejects what he calls "the termination thesis," that "when they die, things simply cease to exist" (1992, 104). "[W]hen a living thing dies," he says, "it ceases to exist *as a living thing*. . . . But since I think that living things . . . are certain material objects, and I think these material objects persist (as corpses) for at least a little while past their deaths, I am not prepared to accept any interesting version of the termination thesis. . . . The good news is that most of us will

2. Henceforth, I won't in general continue to add an asterisk when speaking of essence. I will assume the context will make clear which sense of essence is at issue, or that the distinction is not relevant.

survive death. . . . The bad news is that . . . each of us will then be dead" (105). In support of his position, Feldman marshals ordinary language evidence, for example, "We often say such things as that Aunt Ethel died last week and we're burying her tomorrow" (94). Indeed, after the funeral, relatives may come from miles away to see the place where Aunt Ethel is buried. After all, why do we engage in the respectful ceremony of burying the dead if the dead we're burying aren't the ones we love? One could supply many such examples. Do the police not say such things as that "poor Smith was found stabbed to death sitting at the desk in his study?" And so on.

Feldman is not alone. Judith Jarvis Thomson, in "People and Their Bodies," advances a similar view. "Suppose," she writes, "Alfred and Bert are people who die of a disease, in their beds. Their bodies did not go out of existence at that time. So if Alfred and Bert went out of existence at that time, then they are not their bodies. But did Alfred and Bert go out of existence at that time? Don't people who die in bed just become dead people at the time of their deaths? Cats who die in bed become dead cats" (1997, 155).

One must admit that as Feldman and Thomson suggest, there is evidence from ordinary language for their position. At the same time, there's evidence from ordinary language against their position. We say that poor Smith, who just died, has finally left us. If you haven't heard the sad news about Smith and enquire if he's still with us, you won't be told that yes, indeed, he is, only now he's a corpse. The inconclusiveness of the linguistic evidence, I believe, is due to the fact that most people (including most philosophers) simply don't know what to say about the dead and, more generally, about the nonexistent. What makes things even more confusing is that there are as many ways to cease to exist as there are kinds of beings, hence, kinds of essence, indeed, many ways to cease to exist even for one and the same kind of being. If, let us suppose, the essence of an *auto*mobile is the power of self-movement, then if your car is beyond repair, even if it remains bodily intact, it has lost this power, and thus ceased to exist, no less than if it had been obliterated by a bomb. Yet although it would unsurprising if your neighbor informed you that her car stopped running years ago, it would be odd indeed if she told you that her car had long since ceased to exist, when what looks to all the world like her car—albeit in poor repair—sits in the driveway. Yet the "corpse" of a car, so to speak, is no more a car than the corpse of Socrates is Socrates.[3]

---

3. It doesn't follow, of course, that a car isn't a physical object, nor that you aren't identical with your body. Yet Kripke cites a familiar line of argument. "Let 'A' be a *name* (rigid designator) of Descartes's body.... [P]rovided that Descartes is regarded as having ceased to exist upon his death, 'Descartes ¹ A' can be established without the use of a modal argument; for if so [i.e. if Descartes ceased to exist upon his death], no doubt A survived Descartes when he was corpse. Thus A had a property ... which Descartes did not. The same argument can establish that a statue is not a hunk of stone" ("Identity and Necessity," in A. W. Moore 1993, 191, note 20). If Descartes = A, however, even if Descartes ceased to exist upon his death, it doesn't follow that A survived Descartes's death. Perhaps *a* body, his corpse—let's name it "C" —survived his death, but on the assumption that Descartes = A, *the* body that = Descartes, namely, A, did not survive his death. A ≠ C.

A and C are "congruent" but not identical bodies. They have different identity conditions. What destroys one does not destroy the other. (See Richard Sharvy [1969], "Things," especially section 5: "Identity, Congruence, and Ontology.") A full discussion would need to invoke Aristotelian distinctions between matter, form, essence, accident, and substance, i.e. what Quine referred to disparagingly as the jungle of Aristotelian essentialism. As Sharvy notes, however, "if this is a jungle, it is one that we all live in" (502). One path in this jungle stands out clearly, that

The fact is, we simply aren't used to evaluating the world *from an ontological point of view*,[4] and thus our attitude to the nonexistent tends to be confused. Facts of ordinary usage can't always be relied on. In the case of Feldman and Thomson, we have to make a decision as to which linguistic evidence we find more compelling, which linguistic evidence matches up with our considered ontological reflections. For myself, Kripke's imagined dialogue in "The First Person" about death and survival, though brief, hits home: "Descartes, I say, was not identical to his body when his body was a corpse. 'Descartes had a serious accident, did he survive?' 'Yes, of course—take a look in his coffin.' The response is absurd" (2011, 310).

Equally compelling is Steven Luper's reply to Feldman in *The Philosophy of Death*: "If I am in a morgue," he writes, "and someone asks, 'How many dead people are here?', it is true that I will start counting corpses. If I am asked, 'How many dead people can you name?', I will not count corpses.

one should not confuse the *matter* of a body with the body that is *made of* this matter. Although A ≠ C, A and C may be made of the same matter.

To be sure, Kripke goes on to say that one could maintain that "a person exists if and only if his body exists and has additional physical organization," but that "[s]uch a thesis would be subject to modal difficulties similar to those besetting the ordinary identity thesis." This conflicts, however, with his statement referred to above that "'Descartes ≠ A' can be established *without* the use of a modal argument." The modal argument turns out to be essential. Feldman and Thomson, in turn, who maintain that Descartes = his body, should not have argued that if Descartes is survived after his death by his corpse, he continues to exist, without demonstrating that Descartes's corpse = his body.

4. As Sharvy says, "Describing these situations in the language of quantificational logic requires that we analyze the situations *ontologically*" ("Things," 499; emphasis added).

One dead person I can name is Socrates, and it is clear, in his case, that I am not naming his remains, which ceased to exist long ago. I do not call him a 'dead person' while he is a corpse and not after the corpse disintegrates" (2009, 46).

One could continue this debate further, but for myself, what Kripke and Luper say in favor of "the termination thesis" and against Feldman and Thomson is decisive. You will not survive your death as a corpse. When death comes, you go. And since you'll no longer be here to be buried, it follows that you can't be buried.[5] You can't put what doesn't exist into a grave—not even a very shallow one. Paradoxically, only the living can be buried. This leaves us, however, with the question: Why do we bury, with so much ceremony, the bodies of the dead, if it's not the dead themselves we're burying, but only their corpses? One could cite health considerations, as well as considerations of space, and, of course, reasons having to do with religion. I think the Bible is indeed at the heart of this custom, but not directly, not in virtue of the biblical view that we're God's creatures. I'm thinking, rather, of what I call *Hebraic morality*,[6] in particular, with the proscription in the Hebrew Bible, Exodus 23:19: "Do not boil a kid in its mother's milk." What is the basis of this proscription? Biblical scholars debate the point, but to my mind, it's hard to deny that there's a suggestion here that it's somehow "unfitting" to employ the food of life of a living being in order to benefit from its death, in particular, when that food is provided by the very being that brought life in the first place. It's wrong, that is, but it's not exactly a question of ethics, in

5. See "Can the Dead Really Be Buried?" (Yourgrau 2000).

6. I developed this notion in 1977, when writing a predissertation "proposition" on abortion when I was a graduate student at UCLA.

any of the traditional senses of morality we recognize today. For example, it doesn't involve a violation of anyone's rights. Nevertheless, I'm inclined to speak of Hebraic *morality*, a conception of right and wrong that's of independent interest, however one interprets the Biblical text.

Once one has grasped the idea, I've noticed, one begins to recognize Hebraic morality in many contexts. It seems to account, for example, for the story of G. K. Chesterton, who, finding himself alone in a railway car with the body of a dead man, chose to put out his cigar. "There was something unnecessarily horrible," he wrote, "in the idea of there being only two men on that train, one of them dead and the other smoking a cigar." Chesterton certainly didn't believe he was violating the rights of the corpse, but all the same, he felt there was something amiss about smoking a cigar while accompanying the body of a dead man.[7]

For myself, recently, I think I recognized it in the story of why former First Lady Barbara Bush, whose hair turned white while nursing her daughter to the end of her fatal illness, chose not to dye it back to its original color. It was out of respect for her daughter, some commentators said. This sounds right, but I would also say that we appear to have here another example of Hebraic morality. For Barbara Bush, perhaps, it would have been somehow "unfitting" or "inappropriate"—an offense, as it were, against the nature of things—for her to return her hair to the condition it was in before her daughter's sad death before her eyes.

In the case before us as to why we "bury the dead" with such dignified ceremony if it's only a corpse we're really burying, the answer, I believe, is that Hebraic morality counsels

7. Thanks to Ben Callard for drawing my attention to this story.

us to *respect* the body which once housed a human soul—
or if we don't believe in souls, to respect a body that, if not
identical to the person who died, is "materially equivalent"
with the person before they died. Similarly, we don't, at the
death of one's father, chop up his favorite rocking chair for
firewood, and don't grind up his corpse for fertilizer or throw
it onto an ash heap, and not, *pace* Feldman and Thomson, because the corpse really is our dead father himself. When one
is horrified by images of war crimes involving corpses of slain
victims tossed into mass graves as one would throw out the
trash, this is another example of the pull of Hebraic morality.
Indeed, surely a not insignificant component of the crime of
the Holocaust consists not only in the killing of innocents
(examples of which, sadly, abound in human history), but in
what's often called the dehumanization of the victims—an
extreme violation of Hebraic morality, made even worse by
being inflicted on the descendants of the very people who
gave the world this morality.

Perhaps, though, even if Feldman's and Thomson's
arguments against "the termination thesis" are ultimately unconvincing, the very idea that at death and consequent nonexistence you lose your life but not your essence is simply
misguided. Perhaps, as many philosophers seem to think,
you simply "disappear" when you die, "erased" from the
framework of reality as one would rub out a drawing on the
blackboard. As should be clear by now, however, I think it
would be a serious mistake to think this way. *Time* magazine, as discussed earlier, had it right when it represented the
death of bin Laden, hence, his nonexistence, with a picture of
him on the cover, crossed out with a big X. If you're lecturing
on the capture and killing of bin Laden, you might draw a
picture of him on the blackboard, and then conclude your

lecture by drawing, as *Time* did, a big X across that drawing. That would be the right thing to do. The wrong thing to do would be to simply erase the drawing, to rub it out. A blank blackboard does not represent the death of bin Laden. On the contrary, it represents nothing, but bin Laden, on dying, did not become nothing, just as he did not come from nothing. (*Ex nihilo, nihil fit*, as I remarked earlier.)

Just this, however, seems to have escaped many, if not most philosophers who've written about the metaphysics of death. Shelly Kagan, for example, writes in his popular study *Death* that "nonexistence is nonexistence. It's no kind of condition or state that I am in at all [after I've died]" (2012, 323). Kagan seems to believe that when you've died and ceased to exist, there's "no one left" to be in any sort of state or condition. There's no one left even to be in the state of nonexistence, to have the property of nonexistence. He seems to subscribe to Quine's doctrine that "in our common-sense usage of 'exist', that [bin Laden] doesn't exist, means simply that *there is no such entity at all*." If there's no such entity, obviously, there's no such entity to occupy the state of nonexistence, to have the property of nonexistence.

As I said, this is a widely held view among philosophers of death. To choose another prominent example, consider what Francis Kamm writes in *Morality, Mortality*: "[L]ife can sometimes be worse for a person than the alternative of nonexistence, even though nonexistence is not *a better state of being*" (1993, 15–16; emphasis added). For Kamm, nonexistence is never a *better* state of being than is existence because for her, apparently, nonexistence is not a state of being *at all*.

Kamm and Kagan, however, are mistaken. What they say is true not of Socrates but of the tooth fairy. The tooth fairy is indeed not in a state of nonexistence for the simple reason that *there is no such person as the tooth fairy*. By contrast, there is such a person as Socrates. Salmon, in "What Is Existence?," puts the matter succinctly: "'Kripke exists' is true whereas 'Napoleon exists' is false. Kripke has existence. Napoleon has nonexistence" (251).

When you die and cease to exist, you aren't "erased," you aren't "rubbed out,"[8] nor do you turn into a different kind of being. You forfeit your existence, not your essence. Death affects *that* you are, not *what* you are. Thus, assuming, for the sake of argument, that persons are concrete objects and that that is part of their essence, when Socrates died he didn't cease being concrete. He went from being *an **existent** concrete object* to being *a **nonexistent** concrete object*. And the same is true, analogously, of an inorganic concrete object like a rock. This will no doubt sound paradoxical (not to say, downright crazy) to many people. Surely, what's not there can't be *concrete*! After all, if something's concrete, you can trip over it in the dark, whereas there's no need to worry about tripping over the nonexistent. True enough, if we're speaking about an actual, an *existent* concrete object. But here we're speaking of concrete objects that have ceased to exist—i.e. that have lost their existence, but not their essence. (Indeed, what would it mean for something to lose its essence? What would make it that very thing that had lost

8. I can't help but be reminded here of what the Cheyenne Indian chief, Old Lodge Skins, said to Dustin Hoffman's character in the film *Little Big Man*, about what happened when the members of his tribe (whom he calls "the Human Beings") went out on a war party against the Pawnees, who were too many for them: "One by one, the Human Beings were rubbed out." (You can find the script here: http://www.script-o-rama.com/movie_scripts/l/little-big-man-script-transcript.html.)

it?)[9] The moral, then, is this: *Concreteness should not be confused with actuality.*

Please don't think I'm picking on Kagan and Kamm. They're no different than most philosophers who believe that death implies nonexistence in failing to appreciate the fact that they are then faced with the paradox of nonexistence and the problem of the predicate of existence.[10] To be sure, the so-called no-subject problem has been the source of considerable debate, but the focus there has been confined to the question of whether death can be harmful given that there is "no subject left" to suffer this harm, in particular, no subject left to experience any harm, given, for example, the principle Harry Silverstein puts forward which he entitles "Values Connect with Feelings" (1993, 107, note 12). The question of the ontological status of the dead, qua nonexistent, has simply not been an issue. After all, the feeling seems to be, what more needs to be said than, as Kagan put it, "nonexistence is nonexistence"? Every effort has been made to avoid talking about, referring to, the dead

9. As will be seen later, however, this hasn't prevented Niall Connolly from maintaining in "How the Dead Live" (2011) that at death one loses both one's existence and one's essence and becomes a mere "bare particular."

10. Harry Silverstein, in "The Evil of Death" (1993), like most philosophers of death, believes that "a dead person no longer exists," but unlike most others, he addresses the metaphysics of the situation. His approach involves endorsing so-called four-dimensionalism, so that, by his lights, although Socrates no longer exists in the sense that he does not share our location in the four-dimensional space-time continuum, in a tenseless sense, he has never ceased to exist, since, like all four-dimensionalists, he believes that location in that continuum does not determine what exists from a tenseless point of view. *Where* you are in the space-time continuum does not determine *whether* you are. I'll be discussing this approach later on.

themselves, the nonexistent.[11] That's why, paradoxically, so much that's been written about the harm of death has been centered on the question of whether and how death affects the living person, *ante mortem*. Isn't it obvious, however, that it's *the dead* person who is suffering the greatest harm from his death?[12]

This difficulty of speaking coherently of the dead is by no means confined to philosophers of death, nor, indeed, to philosophers of any stripe. It's especially noticeable in book dedications, where authors simply cannot bring themselves to refer to the dead, themselves, substituting instead reference to *the memory* of the dead. When you think about it, however, this is absurd. Unlike the dead, our memories of the dead are alive and well, and in any case, are a poor substitute for the loved ones being honored in the dedications. It's your mother who taught you to love music, not your memories of your mother, your father who first took you to a poetry reading, not your memories of your father, and so on. What could be more different from a *dead* parent than a *living* memory? The nonexistence of the dead should make us more attuned to what's real, not less. For the dead relative is every bit as *real* as, though less *existent* than, the living memory. "Never . . . think of a thing or being we love but have not actually before our eyes," Simone Weil wrote in *Gravity and*

---

11. As indicated in the previous note, Silverstein is unusual in being willing to refer to the dead themselves, but for him this is possible because he believes that from a tenseless point of view, the dead are not nonexistent.

12. The reluctance to speak of the dead themselves is so great that it has been proposed that it's the survivors who are the real victims of death. As I wrote in "The Dead," however: "The grievers grieve over the misfortune of death. Death is not a misfortune because it gives rise to so many unhappy grievers" (Yourgrau 1993, 140).

Grace,[13] "without reflecting that perhaps this thing has been destroyed, or this person is dead. May *our sense of reality* not be dissolved by this thought but made more intense. . . . *Love needs reality*" (14 & 57; emphasis added).

Yet, when I take a look, randomly, at books on my shelves, I see dedication after dedication not to the departed, themselves, but only to memories of the departed. I've discovered no exception to this curious fact. Only a long list of dedications can give you an idea of how striking this phenomenon is, so here, arranged in no particular order, is such a list: Ludwig Wittgenstein, *Tractatus Logico-Philosophicus* (1961): "Dedicated to the memory of my friend David Pinsent"; Shelly Kagan, *Death* (2012): "This book is dedicated to the memory of my parents"; Gregory Vlastos, *Platonic Studies* (1981): "To the memory of Vernon Abbott Ladd Vlastos"; Eli Hirsch, *The Concept of Identity* (1973): "To the memory of Dean Kolitch"; D. H. Mellor, *Real Time* (1981): "To the memory of F.P. Ramsey"; Charles Parsons, *Mathematics in Philosophy* (1983): "To the memory of my father"; Crispin Wright, *Frege's Conception of Numbers as Objects* (1983): "The book is dedicated to the memory of my friend, the late Gareth Evans"; Gershom Scholem, *Major Trends in Jewish Mysticism* (1995): "To the memory of Walter Benjamin"; Michael Hallet, *Cantorian Set Theory and Limitation of Size* (1984): "To the memory of my father"; Richard Tieszen, *After Gödel* (2011): "To the memory of Hao Wang (1921–1995)"; Paul Wiljdeveld, *Ludwig Wittgenstein: Architect* (2000): "To the memory of my father, and to my mother"; Peter van Inwagen, *Material Beings*

13. Weil 1992. See, further, my book *Simone Weil* (Yourgrau 2011).

(1990): "To my mother, and to the memory of my father"; Michael Beaney, *The Frege Reader* (1997): "To Peter Geach and to the memory of Max Black."

Note how distinguished are the writers on this list. Note also how sometimes a book is dedicated to one parent and then only to the memory of the other, or to one colleague and then only to the memory of the other. Why not simply dedicate the book to both parents and to both colleagues? To be sure, there are dedications where the author says, "in memory of *x*," which is better, but still, why bring in memories at all? Why not dedicate the book simply to *x*? Indeed, the very phrase, "dedicated to the memory of *x*" refers to *x*! So, again, why not refer simply to *x*? Why else, surely, but for the fact that the paradox of nonexistence, in one of its varieties, has a tight grip on thinkers of all kinds? How peculiar, then, that philosophers of death, who have recognized that death means nonexistence, should have neglected this paradox, along with the puzzling predicate of existence.

Talk of the dead, of the nonexistent, even with the best of intentions, is indeed awkward. Kripke, for example, confesses in *Reference and Existence* that " 'Moses, Napoleon, no longer exists' strikes me as true, and expressing the fact that the individual referred to is dead, no longer with us, even though he once was. To my ear, the simple 'Moses (Napoleon, etc.) does not exist' is not the best way to express the matter. In my own discussions, I always imagine the question as being whether the entity *ever* existed" (5, note 6). I agree that the bare statement, "Napoleon doesn't exist" puts one in mind of such assertions as "Santa Claus doesn't exist," which is not the intended analogy. To deny that Santa Claus exists would typically be understood to mean that there is no such person, whereas what one wants to say about Napoleon is that there is such a person, who lacks, however, the property of existence. These are, to my ear, however, questions of pragmatics, not semantics, questions relating to what Paul Grice calls "conversational implicature." If, however, in lawyerly mode, I put the question to Kripke: "Yes or no: Does Napoleon exist?" I expect the answer to be no. The other options, yes, or I don't know how to answer, would be unacceptable.[14]

Experience has taught me, however, that most people simply refuse to agree to the statement that Napoleon doesn't exist, accepting only the statement that Napoleon no longer exists. When, even after I've explained the question of pragmatics, I still can't get someone to agree that Napoleon doesn't exist, I suspect that Parmenides's paradox of nonexistence is at work. Somehow, people believe that saying that Napoleon no longer exists keeps the French general inside the framework of reality. He's not "here and now," to be sure; he's simply "located" in the past. For four-dimensionalists like Quine, Silverstein, and Theodor Sider,[15] this is literally true, but for others, it represents, rather, a convenient way to avoid confronting head-on the paradox of nonexistence, to

---

14. Kripke spoke even more awkwardly about the dead in a much earlier "Second General Discussion Session" (1974b) with Quine, Michael Dummett, Gilbert Harman, and David Lewis, in which he said that "a sentence containing a proper name expresses a proposition if and only if the name has reference" (510). He went on to illustrate his point by saying that "if Moses doesn't exist, people can't use that sentence to express a proposition" (510). Apparently Kripke forgot that since Moses is dead, he doesn't exist, which means that if his thesis were true, his sentence containing the name "Moses" couldn't be used to express a proposition. Indeed, if you combine the two sentences, it would appear that Kripke was conflating referring with referring to something existent. (See "Kripke's Moses" [Yourgrau 2013].)

15. See his study *Four-Dimensionalism* (Sider 2003).

avoid facing up to Quine's challenge that "Nonbeing must in some sense be, otherwise what is it that there is not?"

In contrast to Kripke, Kaplan has no problem saying straightforwardly that past objects like the dead don't exist. "Past individuals," he says in "Afterthoughts," "are . . . in my view nonexistent" (1989, 607, note 101). He speaks also of "future individuals and merely possible individuals. Such putative individuals are *nonexistent*" (607, note 101). He has no qualms about quantifying over nonexistent objects. What, then, is the ontological status, according to Kaplan, of such nonexistent objects? As we saw earlier, Salmon, too, recognizes the nonexistent, but it was difficult to determine how exactly to characterize his recognition of them. Kaplan, by contrast, is more forthcoming. "It would . . . be natural," he says, "to add a *narrow existence predicate* to distinguish the robust being of true local existents like you and me from *the more attenuated being of the nonexistents*" (608; emphasis added). Kaplan appears to recognize the fact that in some sense "there are" nonlocal beings, unlike you and me, namely, past, future, and merely possible individuals who, though they don't possess existence (or at least, not "robust" existence), nevertheless have some ontological status, namely, "an attenuated being." What can this "attenuated being" be? It sounds a lot like what I've been calling *being*—though it's not entirely clear whether Kaplan's "attenuated being" is to be understood as an attenuated form of *existence*. Nevertheless, whether or not Kaplan is going all the way, he appears to be moving in the direction of something like Russell's distinction between being and existence.[16]

---

16. Indeed, Kaplan has claimed that in some circumstances we can uniquely identify particular merely possible individuals: "In the most

Clearly, Kaplan, Salmon, and Kripke are on the front lines in the attempt to make logical sense of the predicate of existence and the enigma of nonexistence in the context of foundational issues in QML and the New Theory of Reference. Yet most philosophers on the front lines of the philosophy of death have almost completely failed to engage with these logico-semantic investigations of Kripke, Kaplan, Salmon, et al. Indeed, to a considerable extent, the reverse is also true. The left hand doesn't know what the right hand is doing. With the exception of my own work,[17] it seems, the question of nonexistent objects does not so much as arise in the field of the metaphysics of death,[18] even though, as we've seen, with a few notable exceptions, that death means nonexistence is accepted by nearly all workers in the field. "Death means nonexistence"—fine. "The dead are nonexistent objects"—absurd! Meinongianism!

One might perhaps have thought, however, that when I attempted in my contributions to demonstrate to the left hand what the right hand was doing (or vice versa), that might have inspired the beginning of mutual engagement. Quite the reverse, however, has happened. Consider the example of Silverstein, one of the leading contemporary

plausible cases we speak of the unique possible individual that would have resulted had a certain closed, developing deterministic system not been externally aborted" ("Bob and Carol and Ted and Alice," Kaplan 1973, 516–17). Salmon has argued similarly in "Nonexistence" (2008c, 61).

17. "The Dead" (Yourgrau 1993); "Can the Dead Really Be Buried?" (Yourgrau 2000); "Kripke's Moses" (Yourgrau 2013).

18. Thus, in the seminal collection of essays assembled by John Fischer, *The Metaphysics of Death* (1993), every entry in the index under "nonexistent object," without exception, refers to my contribution, "The Dead."

philosophers of death.[19] In "The Evil of Death Revisited," he is so exasperated by my writings on death that he says, "I cannot forebear noting that Yourgrau's views in general are exceedingly strange" (2000, 132, note 12). What are these "exceedingly strange" views?

To begin with, according to Silverstein, there is the fact that "[Yourgrau] defends a neo-Meinongian outlook according to which the existential quantifier ranges over 'being' rather than 'existence', 'existence' being just one property among others (though his Meinongianism is a parsimonious one in which some 'things'—for example, Pegasus—are not given even the status of 'being')." There are a number of important points here that need to be taken up. Silverstein is far from alone in harboring these misgivings, and the clarification of what's going on here is crucial to a proper understanding of my position. To begin with, he's perfectly right that my ontology of the dead is a radically unfamiliar one in the field. He's mistaken, however, in describing it as "neo-Meinongian." As I've emphasized in the preceding pages, although I believe the dead are nonexistent objects, my reasons for countenancing nonexistent objects, my views about what they are and which objects there are that are nonexistent, have nothing to do with Meinong. As I've stressed, I reject entirely what I've called Meinong's "semantic naiveté," his belief (shared, apparently, by Russell in 1902) that all singular terms, as such, succeed in referring, if not necessarily

19. Indeed, Silverstein is the one of the few philosophers of death who have taken seriously the task of developing an ontology of the dead. It's no accident that in Theodore Sider's contribution to *The Oxford Handbook of Philosophy of Death*, "The Evil of Death: What Can Metaphysics Contribute?" (2013), the two philosophers of death he singles out for discussion of the metaphysics of death are Silverstein and myself.

to something that exists. There is no simple semantic algorithm for deciding which terms refer to nonexistent objects any more than there is for deciding which terms refer to existent objects.

That's why my supposed "Meinongianism" is "a parsimonious one." One must decide on a case-by-case basis which terms refer to genuine beings, existent or not. We know, for example, that "Socrates" has a referent, albeit a nonexistent one, since we know that Socrates used to exist, though he's now dead, hence nonexistent. By contrast, we know (I am assuming) that "Pegasus" and "Aphrodite" are names used in ancient myths to *pretend* to refer.[20] As such, they refer to nothing,[21] not even to something that happens to be nonexistent. To repeat: a philosophy that can't distinguish between Socrates and Aphrodite can't be right. Yet Silverstein takes me to task precisely for distinguishing between Socrates and Aphrodite—between the dead and the mythical![22]

---

20. Even if you believe the ancient Greeks weren't merely pretending to refer to Aphrodite, you will, I assume, agree that their attempt to refer to a genuine being failed. They didn't succeed in referring to something that merely happens not to exist.

21. To sure, fictional realists like Kripke and Amie Thomasson believe that when *we* use the term "Aphrodite," we refer to an abstract entity, a character created by the mythmakers, not a Greek goddess. But of course, on this use of the name, Aphrodite *exists*.

22. Sainsbury, unfortunately, appears to conflate the dead and the mythical. He writes, for example, that "it's hard to resist inferring from the many examples of things that don't exist that *there are things that don't exist*. Yet . . . it's not that there are dragons having the strange property of nonexistence, it's just that there are no dragons" (*Fiction and Fictionalism*, Sainsbury 2010, 117; emphasis added). I agree with Sainsbury about dragons, but at the same time I'm disconcerted by the fact that he seems unable to distinguish, among "things that don't exist," dead people from

I reject, also, Meinong's principle that *F(the F)* (as do Salmon and Williamson,[23] who may also appear to be Meinongians).[24] My thesis that the dead are nonexistent objects has nothing whatsoever to do with Meinong's round squares and golden mountains. I appreciate, therefore, Sider's pointing out in his article "The Evil of Death: What Can Metaphysics Contribute?" that "[Yourgrau's] distinction between being and existence is in the tradition of Meinong and [Terence] Parsons (1982), but differs importantly since Yourgrau rejects incomplete and impossible objects, and argues for his view on metaphysical, not semantic grounds" (2013, 164, note 9). Still, I can't agree that my views are "in the tradition of Meinong," since the tradition of semantic naiveté—which I reject—according to which every singular

dragons. Napoleon, surely, is an example of a thing that doesn't exist, and, *pace* Sainsbury, it *does* follow from this example that there are things that don't exist. And what's this about "the strange property of nonexistence"? Does Sainsbury wish to deny there is such a property? Or to insist that nothing, including Napoleon, has it? Recall what Salmon said: "Kripke has existence. Napoleon has nonexistence" ("What Is Existence?," 251).

23. "I have often heard the two theories," writes Williamson, "[mine, necessitism, and Meinong's] conflated in discussion, but they have little in common. One of Meinong's most distinctive principles is the notorious characterization schema 'The F is an F' (except for a few tricky substitutions for 'F'). Necessitism is committed to no such principle" (*Modal Logic as Metaphysics*, 2013, 19). Salmon, similarly, in "Nonexistence," denies his approach is Meinongian, despite his belief not only in nonexistent but even impossible objects.

24. Why do I use the strong term "accused," since there are today a number of respected philosophers and logicians who are self-declared neo-Meinongians? I use this term because, generally speaking, in spite of this fact, Meinong remains a philosophical bête noire, and more specifically, because philosophers of death like Silverstein are clearly using the term "Meinongian" as a pejorative; else why would he declare, "I cannot forebear noting that Yourgrau's views in general are exceedingly strange"?

term, as such, succeeds in referring, the tradition that accepts the principle that **F (the F)**, is surely at the heart of Meinong's approach. To be sure, I countenance nonexistent objects, but I think it's misleading to say, on the basis of that alone, that my views (and Salmon's, and Williamson's) are "in the tradition of Meinong."

As to Silverstein's complaint that among my "exceedingly strange views" is my view that "the existential quantifier ranges over 'being' rather than 'existence,'" I've discussed at length, previously, the prominence of the distinction between being and existence, both historically and among contemporary philosophers and logicians. My employment of it in discussing the metaphysics of death may be novel, but the same can hardly be said of the distinction itself. Yet Silverstein, like other philosophers of death, acts if the distinction between being and existence is some strange, unheard-of, new doctrine that fell out of the sky, and which, in any case, has no special relevance to the philosophy of death, even though they acknowledge that death ushers in nonexistence.

David Heyd, similarly, in *Genethics: Moral Issues in the Creation of People*, writes that "Yourgrau's suggestion . . . is based on a mysterious distinction between being and existence (both the dead and the unconceived have being, although they do not exist anymore, or yet, respectively)" (1994, 247, note 31). The left hand, as I said, doesn't know what the right hand is doing. As for what the existential quantifier ranges over, I've discussed previously the views of a number of prominent philosophers and logicians, especially those working on the foundations of QML, according to whom the range of the existential quantifier may extend beyond what actually exists. To cite just one example, here's a reminder of what Kaplan has said: "It is not my claim that the notion of *existence* is captured by the existential quantifier; variables can have any domain" (1989, 611, note 109). Have Heyd and Silverstein never read Kaplan, or Kripke, or Salmon? Or have they read these philosophers but dismissed their views as "exceedingly strange"?

And how about Silverstein's comment that on my view "'existence' [is] just one property among others"? It's not quite clear, I confess, exactly what he's complaining about. Is it simply the idea that existence is a property? Or is it the idea that there's nothing special about the property of existence, that it's just "one property among others"? As to existence being a property at all, I refer the reader to the previous chapter, "The Predicate of Existence," and to the widespread view among leading philosophers of logic like Kaplan, Salmon, Kripke, et al., that, *pace* Frege and Russell, existence is indeed a property of individuals. Has Silverstein somehow missed these important developments in the philosophy of logic? As to whether there's "nothing special" about the property of existence, I remind you of my lengthy discussion, previously, of what Kant had to say about this, and of what I had to say in response to what Kripke, Salmon, and Ishiguro, in turn, had to say about Kant, the upshot of which was not only that existence is a property, but that it's a very special property indeed, in that it separates the existent from the nonexistent, the actual from the possible, even though, as Kant said, "the real contains no more than the possible."

There's more, however, from Silverstein. He objects to my having said in "The Dead" (1993) that "the realm of existence is the merest dot of an 'i' in the vast sea of being." "An implication [Yourgrau] draws," writes Silverstein, "is that the unborn (i.e. those that never did and never will exist) like the dead have 'being' or 'are', and *thus also, like the dead*, 'suffer from the evil of nonexistence.'" Those persons that never did and never will exist are merely possible persons. We're in the territory now of both temporal and modal logic, in particular of QML. Silverstein appears oblivious of debates about the foundations of QML over the question of merely possible individuals. Recall, for example, this comment by Marcus about Kripke's seminal "Semantical Considerations on Modal Logic" to which we drew attention earlier: "In allowing domains of possible worlds," she writes, "to include nonactual individuals, Kripke allows for possibilia. . . . The semantics for Kripke's theory appear to be symmetric between referring to actual objects and referring to possible objects . . . No special problem is noted about assigning possible objects to individual variables serving as individual constants" (1993, 205–6).

Recall, also, my having drawn attention to the fact that Kaplan and Salmon have gone farther even than Kripke did in that early essay, maintaining that in some circumstances one can even uniquely describe particular possible individuals. Silverstein, of course, is free to reject my views about merely possible people, as well as Kripke's, Kaplan's, and Salmon's, but he's not free to fail to note that my "exceedingly strange" views about merely possible individuals, though they're outside the mainstream among philosophers of death, are closely related to ideas in the forefront of discussions of the foundations of QML. An honest criticism of my views would need to widen its target to include the ideas of Kripke, Kaplan, Salmon, et al., which, however, would, I suspect, make it difficult to dismiss this combined approach as "exceedingly strange."

I have a problem, also, with Silverstein's reluctance, together with others in the field, to accept the fact that merely possible individuals fail to exist in exactly the same sense of nonexistence in which past individuals, i.e. the dead, fail to exist. Here I would cite Kagan's comment more positively: nonexistence is nonexistence, whether of past, future, or merely possible individuals. The nonexistence of the dead and the merely possible does, however, differ from the nonexistence of Aphrodite, but that's because it's not really the individual, Aphrodite, herself, who fails to exist, *there being no such person* to either exist, possibly exist, or fail to exist. (Which means, as mentioned earlier, that, as Kripke recognized, the correct analysis of "Aphrodite doesn't exist" is difficult to come by. That's a problem, however, not in ontology but in the philosophy of language.)

At the same time, prenatal[25] nonexistence is also indistinguishable, from an ontological point of view, from posthumous nonexistence, i.e. death, though some philosophers of death have taken me to task for putting forward such a view. David Heyd, for example, in *Genethics: Moral Issues in the Creation of People*, objects that "Palle Yourgrau believes, against Nagel, that inexistence [*sic*] before and after life are ontologically symmetrical and that the only difference between the two is psychological and epistemological (not knowing in advance the identity of the not-yet-conceived-person)" (1994, 246–47, note 31). Of course, the idea that prenatal nonexistence and posthumous nonexistence (i.e. death) are ontologically symmetrical is hardly original with me. It was a central feature of the famous counsel of Lucretius and Epicurus that we should not worry about death, since we're

25. In certain contexts, "prenatal" is used to signify the period during pregnancy before birth. In this study, I use it to represent the period before the person comes to exist, whenever that may be.

not disturbed by our prenatal nonexistence. Heyd mentions Lucretius, yet, for some reason, Lucretius's assumption of "ontological symmetry" does not arouse Heyd's ire. Perhaps the reason can be gleaned from the fact that he goes on to say, as we saw earlier, that "Yourgrau's suggestion . . . is *based on* a mysterious distinction between being and existence " (1994, 247, note 31; emphasis added).[26] This, however, gets things backward. I don't base my observation about ontological symmetry on the distinction between being and existence. I *begin* by noting that symmetry, and then proceed ask how the dead and the unborn can be nonexistent if there's no one "there" to whom the predicate or property of nonexistence applies. (Once again, I note that no such issue arises with regard to Aphrodite.) I conclude that there must, after all,

26. It's not clear to me how Heyd himself can avoid committing himself to something like this "mysterious distinction." "The subjects of genesis choices," he says, "are by definition persons who do not exist" (1994, 97). They are "persons who are possible." (97). Indeed, his entire book concerns such "persons who do not exist," i.e. nonexistents, over whom, it seems, he has no qualms about quantifying. Since his quantifier is not thereby ranging over the existent, however, what exactly is it ranging over? He tells us: the nonexistent. And what exactly is the existential status of the nonexistent that enables them to be quantified over? We're never told.

Is it, perhaps, possibility? If so, is he saying that there *are* people who are merely possible, or that there *possibly are* people who might or might not become existent? He seems to be saying the former, but it's hard to tell . An account of ontological commitment and the range of quantifiers is missing. But he does say that unlike what he calls *potential* people, "people whose existence is dependent on human choice" (97), there are *actual* people, who do not owe their existence to human choice. But, he notes, "This means that actual people do not necessarily actually exist! That is to say, actual people may be either those who exist now, actual living people, or those who will exist in the future, who are not yet living but are going to live anyway" (98). So, on Heyd's view, *are there* both potential people and actual people? Hard to say. Frankly, this all sounds a bit, well, *mysterious*.

be someone "there" in some sense, yet someone who lacks existence. (Recall Quine's statement of Parmenides's paradox of nonexistence.) I then follow tradition by naming the ontological state in which in some sense the unborn and the dead are "there" (to be the subject of the predicate of nonexistence), although nonexistent, "being."

Perhaps what concerns Heyd is not simply the idea of the ontological symmetry between the unborn and the dead, but rather, the idea of the symmetry between the dead and unborn people who never do make it to existence. He has no problem acknowledging the nonexistence of unborn people who come to exist in the future. Indeed, as we've seen, he calls them *actual* people: "actual people may be either those who exist now, actual living people, or those who will exist in the future, who are not yet living but are going to live anyway" (98).[27] Given that I did come to exist, however, I don't see how it can be denied that there always was such a person as me, and that had I not been born, I would have been as nonexistent as I in fact was before my actual birth. If I had not already been possible, if there were not already such a person as me, albeit nonexistent, my birth or conception could not have made me actual. The nonexistence from which I actually arose is no different than the state of nonexistence

27. Heyd's view, here, should be contrasted both with Quine's position and with Thomas Scanlon's. As was noted in the previous chapter, as a four-dimensionalist, Quine believes that past, present, and future people exist equally, in a tenseless sense. From that metaphysical proposition, one can of course draw moral consequences. By contrast, as will be seen in the final chapter, Scanlon advances a strictly moral principle according to which only past, present, and future people can be wronged. That moral principle is consistent with the metaphysical proposition that there are merely possible people who don't, haven't, and never will exist.

I would have been in had I not been born. *Not to exist is not to exist, whether or not it's succeeded by existence.*

The ontology of death or posthumous nonexistence, thus, is intimately related to that of prenatal nonexistence. Indeed, the two states are so closely related that Plato in *The Phaedo* characterizes both as "death," and then proceeds to make what seems like an astonishing claim, that "the living come from the dead, just as the dead come from the living." To many, no doubt, this is just (another) instance of Plato being crazy, or pulling our legs, or telling fairy tales. (Take your pick.) Amusing, perhaps, if you like this kind of thing. For myself, I consider this the first solid beachhead established in the philosophy of death. Since, as the saying goes, no one has ever come back from death to tell us what it's all about, one might think that philosophy has nothing, here, to contribute. Plato, I believe, proves the contrary.

The focus of contemporary discussions has tended to be on Plato's arguments in *The Phaedo* for the immortality of the soul, neglecting thereby his powerful argument from opposites.[28] The basic principle of this argument is: *opposites come to be from opposites.* Call this Plato's Principle of Opposites. Of course, not everything comes to be, in the first place (for example, the number three), but whatever does come to be, must come to be from the opposite state. I've heard this called a "plausible idea." I call it logic. It's no less certain than the principle of noncontradiction, if we assume

---

28. A typical example of this is Kagan's book, *Death* (2012), where he spends a great deal of time on immortality and none at all, as far as I can tell, on the argument from opposites. In person Kagan has informed me that in his lectures he does address this argument. I was glad to hear it, but the fact that he fails to do so in his book is still, I think, telling.

that by "opposites" Plato meant opposites in what we would now call the strict logical sense.[29] How can something come to be F unless it previously was not F? As usual in these contexts, however, there's a question of whether "come to be" is be read as "come to exist," or "come to be F," for some property F. For myself, in the present context, it doesn't matter, though I know that for others, including Aquinas, as will be seen later, it matters a great deal. I take it to have been established in chapter II that there is a predicate or property of existence, *Ex*. We're concerned here with coming into existence, and this can thus be interpreted as coming to acquire the property of existence, *Ex*. The opposite of this predicate or property, then, would be ~*Ex*, being nonexistent.

Before one comes to exist, then, one is nonexistent. No one *knows* you're nonexistent, of course, when you're non-existent. No one says, before Socrates exists, "What a shame Socrates won't exist for many years! We could really use his help right now." To repeat the point, epistemology should not be confused with ontology. There is, however, no standard term for our nonexistence before birth (an interesting fact in itself). Plato calls it "death." From a logical point of view, there's no reason not to do this. The salient feature of death, after all, is nonexistence, a feature shared by prenatal non-existence. Of course, the term "death" typically applies to nonexistence after life, but if our concern is strictly with on-tology, *nothing distinguishes the nonexistence of the unborn from that of the dead.* They're perfectly symmetrical. To quote Kagan yet again, "Nonexistence is nonexistence." Since, at birth or conception, then, one comes to exist, it follows from

29. Though it must be admitted that (for some reason) some of Plato's examples involve contraries.

the Principle of Opposites that *one must previously have
been nonexistent*, i.e. "dead." The conclusion Plato draws is
that "the living come from the dead in this way no less than
the dead from the living" (*The Phaedo*, 72a, transl. Grube).
An extraordinary thing to say, but, I believe, a perfectly correct inference to draw from the perfectly sound Principle of
Opposites.

And look what follows from this conclusion. It's often
asked, can one survive one's death? Plato's answer is of
course! Everyone who exists has already "made the journey"
from nonexistence to existence. Naturally, it doesn't follow
that one will make the journey again, but the question wasn't
will one survive one's death, but is it *possible* to survive death,
i.e. nonexistence?[30] But how, someone may ask, can you be
certain that it's *you* who might survive death again, having already survived "death" by being born? Whatever one makes
of the search for criteria of identity over time (about which
Kripke expressed skepticism in *Naming and Necessity*), what
possible criteria of identity could be employed to make certain Plato is right to identify the nonexistent individual he,
and I, are describing as your prenatally nonexistent self and
also your posthumously nonexistent self? The answer is that

30. There are in fact simple examples of things that have survived nonexistence twice. A soldier's rifle came into existence at one time, emerging,
thus, from nonexistence. Suppose, in a training exercise, the soldier takes
the gun apart, completely, and the sergeant scatters the pieces around
the camp. During that time, the rifle ceased to exist. If you're inclined to
deny this, suppose the pieces are scattered over North America. Now do
you agree the rifle doesn't exist? Suppose now that somehow the soldier
retrieves all the pieces and reassembles the rifle. The rifle has once again
survived nonexistence. (This example, in one form or another, is not original with me. I believe I've heard or read it, or something like it, from various philosophers, not all of whom draw the same moral from it that I do.)

no response is required to the demand for such criteria, since it's the demand itself that should be rejected. The same argument Kripke advanced in *Naming and Necessity* when he denied the need to provide criteria of identity for an individual, *x*, when specifying a possible world as containing *x*, applies here. When I speak of *you* being nonexistent before becoming existent, the presupposition of my statement is that it's *you* I'm speaking about. It would be absurd to demand from me evidence, through the application of criteria of identity, to establish that it was really you to whom I was referring. And the same is true of my references to you during life and after death. The presupposition, once again, is that it's you I'm referring to.[31]

Yet how, then, do we explain, someone might ask, why after the US SEAL team shot the person they thought was bin Laden, they went to pains to identify the corpse as the body of bin Laden, relying on qualitative features of the corpse to make this identification? This question should not be confused with the question I've just been asking. It's one thing to discover, or confirm, that a certain individual, or in this case, a corpse, that you're confronted with in experience or on the basis of descriptive testimony is indeed the one you're interested in, it's another to be asked how you managed to discover that when you state that it's bin Laden who's been

31. This doesn't mean, of course, that if you returned after death, you would necessarily remember who you are. Even if one countenanced criteria of identity over time that required persistence of personal memory, it would make no sense to try to bring those criteria to bear on changes in your existential status. We can "track" an object over time. It makes no sense to speak of "tracking" an object across the journey from nonexistence to existence (and back again), just as it would be senseless to speak of "tracking" an object across possible worlds.

killed, you know you're thereby referring to bin Laden. It's one thing *to discover* if it's bin Laden you've just shot dead, quite another *to succeed in referring* to bin Laden when you announce you've killed bin Laden. Indeed, you can succeed in referring to bin Laden in announcing his death even if you in fact *misidentified* the person you actually shot as bin Laden.

Still, many people, I've found, resist Plato's reasoning here, even though doing so requires believing that one somehow, miraculously, *acquires* existence even though one was not, prior to this, *lacking* existence. They will say that this reasoning is sound in the case of acquiring a property like being rich, but then go on to say that of course existence is *not* a property like being rich. In fact, they say, it's not a *property* at all. When you don't like where modus ponens is leading you, you substitute modus tollens. Since Plato's conclusion would follow if existence were a property, you deny that it's a property. I assume, however, that our discussion of the property or predicate of existence in chapter II short-circuits this line of reasoning.

At this point, I'm inclined to make a nod in the direction of Hume (or perhaps Darwin). No matter the logical force of Plato's reasoning, our natural inclinations are so strong we simply can't bring ourselves to accept his conclusion. After all, if Plato's right, the Brooklyn Bridge—if we take it to be an individual that came to exist[32]—was, before its construction brought it into existence, a nonexistent object, a merely possible bridge. This conjures up a surreal image of a giant, nonexistent bridge of concrete and steel "waiting in the

32. I'll have more to say about this assumption later.

existential wings" (as van Inwagen put it),[33] for its moment to arrive.[34] That sounds absurd. What's absurd, however, is only the *image* that's conjured up of a giant concrete structure floating weightless before gaining weight in Brooklyn.

If, however, Plato's reasoning based on the Principle of Opposites is sound, it follows that our lives are indeed islands of existence surrounded on all sides by nonexistence. Consider, then, the following three existential stages: (1) *Socrates* before birth; (2) *Socrates* during his life; and (3) *Socrates* after his death. What stands out is the fact that one and the same individual, Socrates—the man, not an existential stage of the man—is a *constituent* of all three stages, even though he's *existent* in only one. And note that as just suggested, Socrates is not the same thing as the-existent-Socrates.[35]

Yet careful readers of *The Phaedo* will justly complain that the conclusion Plato actually reaches differs in a crucial respect from my own. The conclusion that Plato actually draws in the dialogue is *not* that before birth we, like the dead, were nonexistent objects, but rather that the common

---

33. *Material Beings*, 1990, 59.

34. Compare the image created by the surrealist painter René Magritte in *Le Château des Pyrénnées*, of what looks like a giant rock floating in midair, with a castle on top.

35. Similarly, Socrates is not the same thing as the-bachelor-Socrates. The latter is not a person but rather a person-stage, like the-young-Socrates. A person is, in Aristotelian terms, a "substance" that retains its identity while changing over time. (Indeed, for Aristotle, that's one of the defining characteristics of a substance.) Socrates, the man, *survives* growing older, whereas the person-stage of his youth—i.e. the-young-Socrates—*ceases to exist*. Similarly, the-bachelor-Socrates can't get married, though Socrates can, and, crucially, for our purposes, *the-existent-Socrates* can't die, though *Socrates* can.

constituent in situations (1)–(3) is Socrates's *soul*, which is thus seen to be *immortal*. And an *immortal* soul, of course, is rather different from a *nonexistent* object! What's going on? What's going on is that by "acquiring existence" Plato means "acquiring bodily existence," and for Plato what acquires bodily existence, what becomes embodied, is the soul. I've made no such assumption, and at the same time, I've offered no argument against Plato's assumption.

Plato, by contrast, argues elsewhere in *The Phaedo* for his.[36] I won't, here, attempt an evaluation of these other arguments. I've been assuming, without argument, that after one dies and before one's born, one does not exist *in any state*, in particular, in a disembodied state, as a soul without a body. By contrast, Plato's assumption that after one dies and before one's born, one exists *in a certain state*, the state of a disembodied soul, is followed up by a series of arguments in favor of this assumption. Our paths diverge, then, not over the question of the soundness of the Principle of Opposites, but rather over the decision to examine the question of the existence of the (immortal) soul. The logic of the Principle of Opposites, however, remains sound, regardless of which assumption about the soul one makes. That's why I credit Plato with having established the basis of my reconstructed argument that the existent "come from" the nonexistent. Moreover, since I presume Plato did not believe that bridges have souls, I can't see how he could resist the conclusion I draw from the Principle of Opposites with regard to nonliving individuals, like the Brooklyn Bridge, and so the postulation of the "weightless" Brooklyn

---

36. As mentioned earlier, Kagan, in *Death* (2012), argues against all of Plato's arguments for the existence of an immortal soul.

bridge, "waiting in the existential wings," must be credited, ultimately, to Plato.

This is all well and good, some will say, yet isn't it obvious that whatever the prenatal nonexistent may be, they're completely different from the dead? Indeed, one of my students[37] at Brandeis University when I last taught *The Phaedo* raised, in one of his papers, with force and clarity, an objection to the suggestion of the categorial identity of the dead and the prenatal nonexistent. Since I suspect his objection would be shared by many, I reproduce it here, with his kind permission. "Those who have lived and died," he wrote, "seem considerably different from those who have not yet or have never lived; the dead have an entire list of actualized traits, *histories*, are unique and form at all times a finite set of objects; the unborn or never born are *unspecific, nameless*, and *infinite* in number. . . . The traits of the dead are *specific*. There is only one dead person who was my grandmother's younger brother . . . [whereas] [t]here are infinitely many younger brothers who never lived. . . . The unborn and the dead, then, are *objects of very different sorts*" (emphasis added).

I will address this type of objection in some detail later on, with regard to the closely related views of Marcus, but let me say a few things right away. To begin with, it should be clear from my description of existential stages (1)–(3) that the name "Socrates" is being used *univocally* in (1)–(3). It's not as if Socrates's prenatal nonexistence presupposes *someone or something else's* nonexistence, from which Socrates's *own* existence emerges, any more than when Socrates dies, it is *someone or something else's* nonexistence that follows. No.

37. Sumner Alperin-Lea.

Socrates's prenatal nonexistence is *his own*, no less than his posthumous nonexistence. The unborn and the dead are *not* "objects of very different sorts" from the living. That's not a hypothesis, nor a guess, a mere epistemological speculation. It's a simple question of logic. It's analogous to the point Kripke made in *Naming and Necessity* regarding transworld identity, which I rehearsed previously. To repeat the point, when I describe a possible world as containing Socrates, there's no need to take a look, somehow, at the possible world *to verify* that it does indeed contain Socrates and not someone who might closely resemble him. The same is true from a temporal point of view. If I speculate about what Kripke was like when he was a child, I don't need to verify that it is the youthful *Kripke* I am referring to (whom I might not be able to recognize), rather than someone I might mistake, based on his looks, for the young Kripke. Similarly, there's no basis to doubt that the coming into existence of Kripke was preceded by the non-existence of *Kripke*, due to the supposed fact that, unlike the living Kripke and (in the future) the dead Kripke, the prenatal, nonexistent Kripke was a mere "unspecific, nameless" entity, "an object of a very different sort" than the actual, living Kripke. *Kripke is Kripke*, whether unborn, living, or dead. As for the question of the prenatal, nonexistent Kripke, unlike the living one, lacking a history, this is an issue I'll be addressing shortly, in my discussion of what Marcus has to say about coming into existence.

IV

THE CLOUD OR

THE RAINDROPS?

The (merely) possible is necessarily general.

—CHARLES PEIRCE

THE ASSUMPTION ON WHICH I'VE been proceeding, that it makes sense to speak of Socrates before he existed, even if only to say that he lacked existence, has been widely challenged, and with it, the conclusion that in being born or conceived, Socrates underwent a *change* from being nonexistent to being existent. No less a philosopher than Thomas Aquinas has rejected both the conclusion and the assumption. Peter Geach, in turn, in *God and the Soul*, has defended Aquinas. Geach quotes Aquinas directly: "In no change is the subject of change produced by the change" (Geach 1969, 71). Why is this? Because "the total production of beings by God, which is known as creation, extends to all the reality that is found in the thing" (71). Hence, "Existence that succeeds nonexistence does not suffice to constitute real change [in the object itself]" (71).

Geach himself attempts to articulate in more modern terms what's behind Aquinas's reasoning. We need to distinguish, he says, "God brought it about that $(\exists x)(x$ is an A)," which is true, from "$(\exists x)($God brought it about that x is an A)," which is false (83). We can then state, he says, for "a suitable interpretation of A," the following: "God brought it about that (∃x)(x is a human soul in body b); and "for no x did God bring it about that x is a human soul in body b" (83). Throughout, the position of the quantifiers is crucial.

The question before us, however, concerns specific *individuals*, like Socrates, whom Geach doesn't mention in his reconstruction of Aquinas's thinking. Putting it in Geach's terms, then, one could say: "God brought it about that (∃x) (x = Socrates)." Socrates, that is, was created, brought into existence, by God. Ipso facto, Socrates did not exist before God created him. After God created him, he did exist.[1] How is this, proceeding from nonexistence to existence, not a *change* in Socrates?

My objection, then, to what Aquinas and Geach are saying is not so much that it's mistaken as that it's incoherent. In Aquinas's own words, Socrates's existence succeeds his nonexistence, which means that he has come-to-be, has

---

1. Rescher, in *Imagining Irreality: A Study of Unreal Possibilities* (2003), provides what he calls a "synopsis" of some of what Aquinas has to say about "things that are not," including the following: "For those things that are not, nor will be, nor ever were, are known by God as possible to his power. Hence God does not know them as in some way existing in themselves, but as existing only in the divine power" (118). Even though Socrates eventually came to exist, surely God did not know him, before he created him, as he existed "in himself," since before God created him, he didn't exist "in himself." Are we not saying, therefore, that before God created Socrates, he didn't exist ("in himself"), but afterward, he did? If so, how does that not represent *a change in Socrates from nonexistence ("in himself") to existence ("in himself")*?

To be sure, one could ask if this was a change in Socrates ("in") himself or only Socrates "in the divine power." Hard to say, but that's not my problem; the distinction is Aquinas's, not my own. On my view, there's only *Socrates*, the self-same being before and after he comes to exist.

come-to-exist, and what is that if not a change in Socrates's ontological status? As Montgomery Furth puts it in *Substance, Form and Psyche: An Aristotelian Metaphysics*, "*If something earlier is not, and later is, then it has come-to-be; that is what coming-to-be IS, from the very meaning of the term, on any 'is' and 'is not' and on any possible account of coming-to-be*" (1988, 194). To sustain his argument, Aquinas is forced to assert that before Socrates came to exist, *it was not a fact about him that he didn't exist*. I, in turn, am forced to reply that it makes no sense to deny that before something came to exist, it was a fact that it failed to exist, from which it follows that coming-to-exist does represent a change in the object itself. In sum, existence that succeeds nonexistence cannot be understood except as coming-to-exist, and coming-to-exist cannot be understood except as *a change from a state of nonexistence to a state of existence*. As Plato said, opposites come from opposites.

Aquinas appears to be concerned that to view coming into existence this way threatens his belief that "the production of beings by God . . . extends to *all the reality* that is found in the thing." And so it does, but at the same time, I don't think this result should be seen to threaten a believer's faith in the supreme ontological status of God. Aquinas is free to believe that ultimately, through the agency of his parents, God alone is responsible for the existence, the *actuality* of Socrates. That doesn't mean, however, that God is responsible also for the *possibility* of Socrates, i.e. for the fact that there is such a person as Socrates to come to exist. But this fact should not be taken to minimize what separates God from his creatures, since Aquinas could still maintain that (a) it is God who is the ultimate cause of the actualization of possibility (as Aristotle, "the" philosopher for Aquinas, believed), and (b) God's possibility, unlike that of his creatures, implies his actuality (the basis, of course, of the so-called ontological argument for the existence of God, an argument, however, about which Aquinas was skeptical). Thomas Nagel, in *The View from Nowhere*, makes dramatic, with regard to (b), how different we are from God. "We are here by luck," he writes, "not by right or by necessity . . . [,] my own existence in particular being one of the most inessential things in the world. Almost every possible person has not been born and never will be" (1986, 211).

Geach is not alone in sympathizing with Aquinas. Arthur Prior has also discussed, favorably, Aquinas's approach to the question of creation. In "Identifiable Individuals," he poses Aquinas's question, "[W]hat was it of which it was possible, before it was made, that it should be made?" (2010, 88), and gives Aquinas's answer: nothing. He quotes Aquinas: "God at the same time gives being and provides that which receives being" (88). He puts Aquinas's way of thinking into his own words: " 'Once X was not, and now it is' cannot mean 'Once X's non-being was the case and now its being is,' but can only mean 'It *is not* the case that X *was*, but it *is* the case that X *is*, and this does not express a change but two contrasting *present* facts (note the tense of the verbs)" (88; final emphasis added). He goes on to say that, for Aquinas, "there can be no question, even for God, of grabbing hold of *Caesar* and bringing him from nothingness to being at some arbitrary time" (89). "Launching Caesar into being," says Prior, considered as a "literal performance, would involve Caesar's existing-before-he-existed. And this seems very close indeed to the admission that *it is only once he exists that Caesar is an identifiable individual*" (89; emphasis added).

My first response to Prior is that the answer to the question, "What was it of which it was possible, before it was made, that it should be made?" is *Caesar*. Nonexistent-Caesar, which, as we saw earlier, is not an individual person, a substance, but rather a person-stage (like unmarried-Caesar or youthful-Caesar), can't come into existence without becoming existent-nonexistent-Caesar, but *Caesar*, the person, not the person-stage, can come into existence. I repeat: we mustn't confuse being an *object* with being *an existing object*. Thus, when Prior says in defense of Aquinas that "there can be no question, even for God, of grabbing hold of *Caesar* and bringing him from nothingness to being," I completely agree, but only because Caesar was never in a state of nothingness. For Caesar to have been in a state of nothingness would have been for Caesar not to have been Caesar, and *Caesar was never not Caesar*. What God was doing, if you believe in divine creation, was rather to grab hold of Caesar (there already being such a being) when he was nonexistent and wrestle him into existence. That doesn't imply, in Prior's words, "Caesar's *existing*-before-he-existed." It implies *there being such a person as Caesar* before he existed.

Failing to invoke the distinction between being and existence, Aquinas and Prior are forced to twist themselves into pretzels to try to make sense of creation. In so doing, they render incomprehensible the very idea of coming into existence. God may well, for believers, be the author of miracles, but creating Caesar out of nothingness isn't one of them. Such creative miracles, moreover, would not be confined to God. If Aquinas's and Prior's account of creation were right, the same kind of miraculous coming into existence from nothing would have to be invoked also for ordinary human creation, like painting a portrait.

Prior, however, doesn't confine himself to explicating and defending Aquinas. In that same essay, speaking for himself, he denies there was such a fact as Socrates's prenatal nonexistence. He employs the highly ambiguous (not to say prejudicial) term "identifiable"—a term born in sin, which blurs the distinction between epistemology and ontology[2]—and asserts that "before Caesar existed . . . there would seem to have been no individual *identifiable* as Caesar . . . who could have been the subject of [the] possibility [of Caesar existing]" (85). Identifiable *by whom*? By us? We *can* (now) identify Caesar as someone who, at that time, had the possibility of existing. We know he was *possible* for the simple reason that we know he became *actual*. By his contemporaries? They, of course, could not have identified Caesar before he existed, but how is their lack of *knowledge* of possible individuals relevant to the question of which possible individuals *there are*? As I've been insisting, to draw an ontological conclusion from an epistemological premise is to commit a philosophical blunder. If, however, the word "identifiable" means only "specifiable," which in turn means only "specific," then

2. Prior is hardly alone in employing the prejudicial term "identifiable." Rescher says that "[u]nactualized possibilities are possibilities for actual things" (2003, 49), whereas "nonexistent possibles . . . or possibilia" are "substances alternative to *real* things," which he describes as "supernumerary items additional to the (real) world's furnishings." He then asserts that "there is no good reason to concede any sort of quasi-existence to such items because . . . such items can never be effectively *identified*" (49; emphasis added). (Adding the term "effectively" gives additional epistemological force to "identifiable.") Further on, he continues in the same vein: "[S]tatements that are ostensibly about nonexistent individuals can—and primarily should—be recast in an informatively equivalent guise without involving themselves in staking claims about nonexistents as *identifiable* quasi-objects" (53; emphasis added).

Prior is not guilty of committing this philosophical sin, but at the same time, he's simply begging the question. (The same alternatives, by the way I believe, hold true of Marcus's critique of Kripke on quantifying over possible individuals in his semantics for QML that I alluded to earlier.)

Curiously, Prior himself goes on to produce a convincing argument that his own assertion must be mistaken, concluding that if his assertion were correct, "there cannot have been at that time [before Caesar was born] any such possibility as that of Caesar's being born to [the parents he actually came to have]. Yet in due course *this non-possible thing actually happened!*" (85; emphasis added). Amazingly, having brought forward a conclusive argument against his prior assertion, he proceeds to *reject* the argument! The rejected argument, however, I want to insist, is perfectly sound. It rests on a principle I believe cannot be objected to without abandoning the very concepts of possibility and actuality, a principle on which I rely throughout this study, namely: *Nothing becomes actual unless previously possible.* Note that the quantifier "nothing" ranges over *individuals.* No thing, no individual thing, x, becomes actual unless it, x, *that very thing*, was previously possible.

I pause for a moment to note the importance, here and throughout this study, of the notion of *individuals*, as opposed to generalities, properties (including "haecceities"), temporal parts, person-stages, four-dimensional space-time worms, infinitely thin three-dimensional slices of four-dimensional space-time, heaps of atoms, or whatever substitutes for individuals have been introduced into the philosophical literature. I assume that proper names like "Arthur Prior," "David Kaplan," "Saul Kripke," etc., refer to individuals. I believe in individual bulldogs, bridges, and buildings. I think philosophers like Derek Parfit who focus on person-stages that have certain relations to other person-stages have brought forth genuine insights concerning the realities of a human life stretched out over time, but I also agree with Nagel in *The View from Nowhere* that Parfit's attempt, for example, to ameliorate the fear of death by focusing only on person-stages is, in the end, self-defeating. As Nagel says, "I actually find Parfit's picture of *survival* depressing. . . . By comparison with Parfitian survival, Parfitian death may not seem so depressing" (1986, 224).

With this in mind, I return to the thesis that nothing—no individual thing—becomes actual unless previously possible. Call this (with apologies to Arthur Prior) the Principle of Prior Possibility. On what basis can Prior reasonably reject this obvious principle of modal logic? The answer is that for Prior, it seems, the realm of mere possibility is like *a cloud before the individual raindrops have formed.* The raindrops, to be sure, in some sense "come from" the cloud, but not because these ("individually identifiable") raindrops were already there, "in" the cloud.[3] Prior cites Charles Peirce, who also appears to believe in the essential cloudiness[4] of the

3. Strictly speaking, at some point, raindrops, or the beginnings of what we see as raindrops, are created inside the cloud. This from "How Raindrops Form" (Brumfiel 2001): "Inside clouds tiny vortices created by the wind spin water-sodden dust particles into clusters, where they meld to form raindrops. . . . Raindrops begin forming when water vapor condenses on micrometer-sized particles of dust floating in the atmosphere. The dust particles grow to millimeter-sized droplets, which are heavy enough to begin falling. As they fall, the droplets accumulate more and more moisture, until they become the large droplets we see here on the ground."

4. Interestingly, Karl Popper refers to Peirce's preference for clouds (of a different sort). "My clouds," writes Popper, "are intended to represent

realm of possibility: "The *(merely) possible* is necessarily *general*, and it is only *actuality*, the force of existence, which bursts the fluidity of the general and produces a discrete unit" (47; emphases added). Call this the Peirce Principle.[5] When it comes to individuals, Prior and Peirce, it seems, would like to *skip possibility entirely and proceed straight to*

physical systems which, like gases, are highly irregular, disorderly, and more or less unpredictable . . . [whereas] a precision clock [is] intended to represent physical systems which are regular, orderly, and highly predictable in their behavior. . . . Peirce conjectured that the world was not only ruled by the *strict Newtonian laws*, but that it was also at the same time ruled by *laws of chance . . .*: by laws of statistical *probability*. This made the world an interlocking system of clouds and clocks, so that even the best clock would, *in its molecular structure*, show some degree of cloudiness. So far as I know Peirce was the first post-Newtonian physicist and philosopher who thus dared to adopt the view that to some degree *all clocks are clouds*; or in other words, that *only clouds exist*, though clouds of very different degrees of cloudiness" ("Of Clouds and Clocks," Popper 1965, 2, 5).

5. There's something similar in mathematics, in relation to the intuitionism of L. E. J. Brouwer, according to which a mathematical statement acquires a truth-value only when actually proved; it wasn't true earlier that it was provable, i.e. possibly proved. Thus Michael Dummett, in *Elements of Intuitionism* (1978), says that, for the intuitionist, " '[w]e *can* prove A' must be understood as being rendered true only by our *actually* proving A" (19). Invoking Plato's dialogue *The Euthyphro*, one could say that what Dummett is asserting is that: p is *provable because proved*, not *proved because provable*. But that means that when an intuitionist sets out to prove a formula, he or she is attempting, *per impossibile*, to prove something (at that time) unprovable.

I believe this constitutes a serious problem for intuitionism, since the Principle of Prior Possibility applies also to the actualization of proofs. I discussed this in "On Time and Intuitionism," an invited talk before the Clavius Group of Catholic Mathematicians at the College of the Holy Cross on July 7, 2015. I thank Mark van Atten for corresponding with me about these issues. I've benefited greatly also from *On Brouwer* (van Atten 2004) and *Brouwer Meets Husserl: On the Phenomenology of Choice Sequences* (van Atten 2007).

actuality, insofar as they deny that the actuality of an individual is preceded by the possibility of that very individual. The Peirce Principle is thus inconsistent with the Principle of Prior Possibility, though, like the latter, Peirce's principle also recognizes the existence of *individuals* (though not their prior possibility). Which principle should be accepted?

The Peirce Principle offers an arresting image—the future solidifying during the march of time like a free-flowing, formless river freezing throughout the winter into solid blocks of ice, generality devolving into particularity. This compelling image, however, must yield to the logic behind the Principle of Prior Possibility, which rests on the very concepts of possibility and actuality. Some questions of modality can be disputed, or admit alternatives. Some cannot. If someone denies that what is necessary is possible, he or she simply fails to grasp the concepts of necessity and possibility. The same is true, I believe, when someone denies that what is actual must have previously been possible. Can we really accept what Prior and Peirce are maintaining, that Caesar, though "nonpossible," somehow managed to become actual—i.e. that *the impossible can become actual*? (I take it that Prior's "nonpossible" can be rendered as "impossible.")

Prior and Peirce, however, are far from alone. Robert Adams in a widely discussed essay, "Time and Thisness" (1989), also, in effect, challenges the Principle of Prior Possibility, though he speaks not of the prior possibility of Caesar existing, but of the prior existence of what he calls Caesar's "thisness," i.e. basically, of the property of being-Caesar. According to Adams, "My thisness, and singular propositions about me, cannot have pre-existed me because if they had, it would have been possible for them to have existed even if I had never existed, and that is not possible"

(26). My response to Prior and Peirce should serve equally as a response to Adams, with suitable changes.[6]

6. Note that if *the possibility of Caesar existing* obtained before Caesar existed, Caesar's "thisness" preexisted Caesar, since, presumably, Caesar can't be possible unless there is such a person as Caesar, and if *there is* such a person as Caesar, there *exists* such a property as being-Caesar, i.e. Caesar's "thisness."

I'm assuming the principle that the property, being-*a* (for some individual, *a*), depends not on the fact that *a exists*, but on the fact that *there is such a person* as *a*. I believe a similar principle holds for sets, the existence of which depends not on the fact that their members exist, but on the fact that there are such things as their members. This conflicts with the standard view that a set exists only so long as its elements exist. Parsons, for example, states, "A well-entrenched principle for talking of sets in modal contexts is that a set exists only if all its elements exist" (*Mathematical Thought and Its Objects*, 2008, 35, note 57) Similarly, Salmon: "Consider any class that has me as an element—{Nathan Salmon}, for example. . . . When I am dead and gone, this class will no longer exist" ("Existence," 2008b, 24).

I believe, by contrast, that it's not the *existence* of its elements that's relevant to the existence of a set, but rather their *being*. It's absurd, I think, to suggest that when the elements of a set die, the set itself "dies" along with its members. Socrates and Plato, during their lifetimes, were obviously not "inside" the set {Socrates, Plato}, the way they were inside someone's home. Imagine if an old-timer, who knew Socrates and Plato, were to say to a young colleague, nostalgically, long after Socrates and Plato had died: "You young people today fail to impress me with your sets. You should have seen the sets that existed in my day." To my ears, at least, that sounds crazy. (I'm reminded of a scene in the movie *Atlantic City* in which Burt Lancaster's character says, "You should have seen the Atlantic Ocean back then.")

Why can't a class, a set, simply acquire new members and thus continue to exist even when its "original members" have ceased to exist? After all, the Supreme Court still exists, even though all its original members have long since ceased to exist. True enough, but a class's members are essential to it, and the Supreme Court is not, in this sense, a *class*. Richard Sharvy has emphasized the distinction between the Supreme Court, which *can* change its members, and the class whose only members are the members of the Supreme Court in year *x*, which *can't*. See "Why a Class Can't Change Its Members" (Sharvy 1968).

In contrast to Adams, Judith Jarvis Thomson, in another widely discussed essay, this time in ethics, "A Defense of Abortion" (1971), doesn't concern herself explicitly with tense and modal logic, but what she says bears directly on the Principle of Prior Possibility. "It is not as if there were unborn persons drifting about in the world," writes Thomson, "to whom a woman who wants a child says 'I invite you in'" (57). To twist a well-known line of Quine's from "Quantifiers and Propositional Attitudes" (1979), one could say that there isn't a specific child "drifting about in the world" that the woman wants to have; she seeks only *relief from childlessness.* "I've decided to go ahead and have a child." "Really? Which child have you decided to have?"

What's problematic, however, is Thomson's saying that "[i]t is not as if *there were unborn persons* drifting about in the world." Forgetting "drifting about," it's simply not true that *there aren't unborn persons.* As I've been insisting: it's an undeniable fact (wherever that fact is "located") that there *is* such a person as Saul Kripke, and an equally undeniable fact that before he was conceived or born, there *existed* no such person. I.e., that prior to Kripke's conception, the following fact obtained (even though no one knew it): *Saul Kripke doesn't exist.* There was, then, such a being as Saul Kripke, an unborn person, a nonexistent object, prior to his conception. And even if one agrees with Salmon (in "Nonexistence") that not all nonexistent objects possibly exist, we know that this particular object, Saul Kripke, did possibly exist prior to his conception, when he was a nonexistent object, for the simple reason that in the course of time he came to actually exist. *What became actual must have been possible.*

Marcus, in turn, focusing her attention on time and possibilia, comes closer than Thomson does to explicitly rejecting the Principle of Prior Possibility. We've already seen some of what she has to say about this in "Possibilia and Possible Worlds" (1993), but let's fill in more of the details. "Suppose I say of a given terrain," she writes, "'There might have been a mountain here.' I might even purport to give it a name, 'Mt. White'. . . . Suppose there is then an eruption and a mountain forms. Could I say that a possible individual, Mt. White, has become actual? Of course not. To be a material object, the object must have had a unique and traceable history in a material order of things. It isn't a thing waiting in the wings to take its place among the actuals when called. There was at the time of 'naming' no history of a definite, albeit, only possible, mountain, such that the very possible mountain that I claimed to name 'Mt. White' was propelled onto the stage of the actual world" (206–7).

We now have the nonexistent pictured "drifting about in the world," "waiting in the existential wings," and "waiting in the wings to take [their] place among the actuals when called." Let's take a look at Marcus's possibilia waiting in the wings. Note first that she doesn't deny that there is an *individual* that comes to exist. She doesn't insist that we should really say only that certain rocks, or atoms, or whatever, came-together-mountain-wise, and so on. She accepts the existence of individuals—in this case, an individual mountain. She accepts that a particular individual mountain that wasn't there beforehand came into existence, became actual. What she denies is that just because that mountain became actual, *it* must have been, previously, a *merely possible individual*. She denies, in effect, that *actualization* consists in *the actualization of the possible*. She denies also that when she supposed there might have been a mountain there, there was a particular mountain she was making that supposition about, a particular mountain she could name "Mt. White."

About the last issue, she's right, but her denial misses the point and muddies the water.

In the event, she supposes that there is an eruption and a particular mountain does form. Marcus doesn't say this, but she could hardly deny that now a particular mountain *is* "identifiable" by her, that now she *is* in a position to name it, say, "Mt. Black." She is now also in a position to assert, truthfully, that since Mt. Black has become actual, *it*—that particular "identifiable" mountain—must have previously been possible. Yet precisely this Marcus fails to do, because she seems to believe that if it *were* true that a particular mountain that was merely possible had become actual, she *should* have been in a position to name it, to identify it, *before* it became actual. But that is simply not true. It's a mistake to suppose that in thinking, "There might have been a mountain here," unless there were a particular mountain she was thinking of, a mountain she would have been in a position to name, if a mountain does subsequently form, it, that very mountain, wasn't already a specific possible object back when she first mused about the possibility of a mountain forming. Marcus misses the fact that after a mountain actually forms, she's now in a *different* position vis-à-vis naming than before that mountain formed. She *can* now name the mountain that actually forms, and she *can* now say truthfully, using the name of that mountain, "Mt. Black", that before that mountain became actual, it was possible—i.e. that before that mountain became actual, it was "waiting in the wings to take its place when called" (though I would still resist speaking of "waiting in the wings").[7]

---

7. Unlike the fact of Socrates's nonexistence before birth, which we were in no position to know, his nonexistence after death is, of course, accessible to us. There are, after all, *death notices* in the obituaries. By contrast, there aren't *nonexistence notices* before birth.

There remains, however, the question of the history of an individual that Marcus raises: "To be a material object, the object *must have had* a unique and traceable history in a material order of things." The man Caesar, after all, had a history, a life filled with many events, most of which appear to have been purely contingent, and which, so to speak, in a sense "define" the man who was Caesar. Surely, no one who lacked that history can be (the historical) Caesar. True enough, but what follows from that? Let's grant that the name "Caesar," by whatever means, as currently used, picks out de facto the man who had such a "unique and traceable history." That man, Caesar, actually existed. But, in spite of the cult of the Roman emperor, he was a man, not a god, not a necessary being, and thus, did not always exist. Before he, Caesar—the man with that "unique and traceable history"—was born, he didn't exist. That is, before the birth of Caesar, Caesar was not an actually existing man. Nevertheless, as we now know, in the course of time, that man, that particular ("identifiable" *by us*, now) individual, came to actually exist. It follows, then, that before Caesar was born, *before he had a history*, he—that very man, Caesar—was possible. The question of Caesar's "unique and traceable history," then, does not represent a challenge to the Principle of Prior Possibility.

If I'm right, however, it looks like I'm left with a seemingly unanswerable question, a question I'm nevertheless always asked: If there was such a person as Caesar before he came to exist and had a "unique and traceable history," what exactly was he *like* before he existed? For many, this question—which is presumed to be unanswerable—is a deal-breaker. If it really was true that it's Caesar himself who was possible before he became actual, nonexistent before he became existent, shouldn't it make sense to ask what he was like before he came to exist, before he became actual? Should I refuse to answer the question, on the grounds that there is simply no such thing as *what Caesar was like when he wasn't*?

Come to think of it, just as it seems not to make sense to talk about what Caesar was like during his prenatal nonexistence, does it not also fail to make sense to ask what Caesar is like right now, during his posthumous nonexistence, i.e. to ask what Caesar's like when he's dead? In point of fact, I believe that both questions do actually make sense and deserve an answer. The key to the answer lies in the fact, alluded to earlier, that one must distinguish the question of *whether* you are from *what* you are, and that what you are, in this context, concerns your essence, not your accidents—not your history over time once you come to exist. Coming into and exiting existence both affect whether you are, not what you are. Just as when you die, you don't become a different kind of thing—a corpse, a memory, or a property like your "haecceity"—when you come into existence, you don't change into a different kind of being. Indeed, if *per impossibile*, in being born and dying you did become a different kind of being, a being with a different nature or essence, it wouldn't be *you* who was born and died.

As to exactly what kind of being Caesar is, this is not the place to attempt a full discussion, but I do need to indicate the kinds of things that might be included in Caesar's nature or essence—i.e. not just those traits he can't lose while continuing to exist, but those traits he can never be without. I think it's safe to say, as alluded to earlier, that Caesar is essentially a living-being (although not essentially alive), i.e. a being for which, in Aristotle's words, "living is existing."

Further, perhaps Caesar is essentially a person.[8] In no possible world is he a tree or a radish or a chipmunk. As to whether he's essentially mortal, I'm not so certain. And whether his essence includes his having the parents he in fact had—a consequence of Kripke's principle of the necessity of origin, put forward in *Naming and Necessity*—is something about which I'm also uncertain. But I think I've said enough to indicate the kinds of things that are included in Caesar's nature or essence. Note that absent from my list so far is precisely what Marcus insisted on: Caesar's "unique and traceable history" as the conqueror of Gaul. Caesar—as Kripke insisted long ago—would still have been Caesar even if he'd never conquered Gaul, even if he'd never written the famous opening words of *The Gallic Wars*: "*Gallia est omnis divisa in partes tres.*"

Another trait that one might want to include in Caesar's essence or nature is being concrete. I don't want to beg the question against dualism of Platonic, Cartesian, or any other stripe, but at the same time, concreteness seems at least a reasonable candidate for inclusion in Caesar's essence. As discussed previously, however, it's easy to misconstrue the idea that mere possibilia can include concreteness as part of their nature, and Luper has indeed misconstrued my suggestion. More clarity, clearly, is needed. In "Nonexistence,"[9] he writes: "Not all concretists accept the view that possibilia exist in other worlds. Palle Yourgrau says [in "The Dead"] that 'possible people, like the dead and the unborn are . . . a

8. It's not clear, however, whether Caesar is essentially a person, in particular, a man. See "Is Socrates Essentially a Man?" (Wetzel 2000).

9. An earlier version of "Never Existing" (Luper 2018) that Luper has kindly given me permission to quote from.

perfectly ordinary kind of concrete object' so he appears to be a concretist. But he also says that 'what separates actual, living people from merely possible people is precisely their existence,' which seems to imply that merely possible people do not exist."

Let me try to unmix what's being mixed up in this critique. In Luper's first sentence, he refers to those "concretists," including myself, who deny that possibilia exist *in other worlds*. Since the very idea of possibilia, i.e. merely possible objects, is that of *objects that exist in other worlds*, it's a mystery why he attributes that denial to me. The mystery is immediately resolved, however, when in his final sentence he correctly attributes to me, in light of the quotation he's just made from my paper, the view that merely possible people *don't exist*. The solution is simple. Merely possible people, I'm saying, who are "a perfectly ordinary kind of concrete object," don't exist—i.e. don't *actually* exist; they merely *possibly* exist, which is to say, they exist only in other possible worlds. What seems to have thrown Luper off is something I suggested earlier, a tendency to conflate *concreteness* with *actuality* or *existence*. Hence Luper's belief that there's a tension between my assertion that possible people are a perfectly ordinary kind of *concrete* object and my view that possible people aren't actual—don't actually exist.

Luper's objection indicates how easy it is to misconstrue the distinction between what you are and whether you are. Kit Fine, fortunately, in "Necessity and Non-existence,"[10] has done much to clarify the situation by invoking a distinction between what he calls worldly vs transcendental properties.

10. In *Modality and Tense: Philosophical Papers* (Fine 2005).

A worldly property is one determined by what happens in a possible world, and "a possible world, in the sense of how things turn out, will . . . be constituted by what exists [in it] . . . [whereas] transcendental properties will be exemplified by objects regardless of how things turn out and so should be taken to be exemplified by objects *regardless of whether or not they exist*" (343; emphasis added).[11] Thus, "[W]hether an object is a man or self-identical is not something that appears to turn on *how things turn out for the object* [i.e. on how the world is]" (336; emphasis added). And so, "[*Socrates's*] *being a man* is an unworldly matter. It is something that holds 'off-stage,' regardless of how things turn out; and so, in particular, it is something that holds *regardless of whether or not he exists*" (338–39; emphases added).

The idea that certain properties are exemplified, certain facts obtain, "off-stage" suggests that, so to speak, the "framework" of possible worlds—"modal space" itself, as it were, as opposed to its occupants, the possible worlds—is something different from possible worlds themselves. As Fine puts it,

---

11. One might think the distinction can't really be made out, since although according to Fine a worldly fact determines, for example, "how things turn out" according to some world, *w*, in particular, *that Socrates happens to exist*, it is at the same time a transcendental fact *that Socrates exists in w*. It's actually a little tricky to sort this out. An analogy might help . *The Great Gatsby* tells us that "Gatsby turned out all right in the end," and students of literature know well that "*The Great Gatsby* tells us that 'Gatsby turned out all right at the end.'" It follow that *The Great Gatsby* does not tell us the same thing that's known by students of literature, since *The Great Gatsby* doesn't tell us that "*The Great Gatsby* tells us that 'Gatsby turned out all right in the end.'" By analogy, it's the job, so to speak, of a possible world to "tell us a story" about how things might turn out. By contrast, it's the job of the transcendental framework of possible worlds to "record the stories" told by each possible world: this$_1$ is how things turn out according to world *a*, this$_2$ is how things turn out according to world *b*, etc.

"A possible world, as so constituted, will only determine the truth-value of certain propositions (or sentences), those that *turn on* how things turn out. . . . The evaluation of an un-worldly proposition, by contrast, will involve no such engagement with the world" (343).

So much from Fine. What does Kamm, who's written extensively about birth and death, think about the personhood of the dead and the prenatal nonexistent? In *Morality, Mortality* (1993) she says, "[S]uppose I am contemplating creating someone I will call Susan and have organized her genetic material so that I know exactly what she will be like. I then decide not to create her. How could there be a harm to her if there never will have been *an actual person*, and therefore *no one* who loses out on all the goods of life?" (24, note 20; emphases added). What's going on here? In the situation envisaged by Kamm, it's not clear if there is or is not a particular person she has in mind whom she can name "Susan." If, as her scenario seems to indicate, the identity of the particular person she would have created if she hadn't changed her mind was fully determined by the genetic setup, then, as Kaplan has noted,[12] she was in a position to name that individual "Susan" and succeeded in doing so. In that case, although Susan was never, as Kamm says, *an actual person*, she was nevertheless a specific *possible person*, a person who has, *pace* Kamm, *lost out on the goods of life*. (I leave aside the question of the morality of depriving Susan of life.)

If, on the other hand, the genetic setup determines "exactly what she [the person who will be created] will be *like*," in a strictly qualitative sense, without thereby determining

12. See chap. III.

her identity as a unique individual, then—assuming there weren't other conditions present that, combined with the genetic setup, fully determined the identity of the person she would have created—it follows that Kamm *wasn't*, after all, in a position to name a unique individual "Susan." Nevertheless, had she not canceled the creation, *some* particular individual would have been created. She would *then* have been in a position to name that person, say, "Alice. The sentence "Alice is a person" could then have been used to express a true proposition (about the referent of the name "Alice"), as could the sentence "If Alice had not been created, she would have lost out on the goods of life." Either way, Kamm is mistaken in concluding that if she cancels the creation, "[there is] no one who loses out on all the goods of life."

We're not done yet, however, with "actual persons." From what Kamm goes on to say, the phrase appears to mean "persons who have actually existed." For Kamm next says, "If we act out of concern for the person that loses goods, we should resurrect someone rather than create someone totally new" (24, note 20). Since, as I've argued, the "someone totally new," whoever that might have turned out to be, who has not been created, is a possible person—a genuine individual, no less than the dead and as yet unresurrected person—the someone totally new is a person who will lose out on the goods of life if uncreated. Hence, "if we act out of concern for the person that loses goods," we can't ignore "someone totally new," in favor of resurrecting the dead.

Kamm, it appears, believes—in company, no doubt, with many philosophers—that having actually existed is a necessary condition for being a person, a view I've been arguing against. At the same time, she appears to agree with me that at least some nonexistents—namely, the dead—are persons. Note also that, ironically, in her view of death and resurrection, Kamm is at one with Plato in *The Phaedo* to the extent of agreeing that at least in certain cases, the living can "come from the dead."

V

WHERE YOU GO WHEN

YOU'RE DEAD

Suppose that (say) Socrates might have lived an additional 10 years. Shouldn't it follow that over the course of the 10 years following his actual death Socrates was an object living outside of the actual world?

—STEVEN LUPER

IT WILL HAVE BEEN NOTICED, or at least should have been, that in the background of my discussion of death and resurrection, of possible people—before life and after death—of essence, of worldly vs. transcendental properties, of nonexistence and nonexistents, and so on is the assumption that possible world talk should be taken seriously. Should it? I've incurred an explanatory debt to the reader that needs to be paid off. And so it will be. But like most debtors, I'd like to put it off for now, to be paid in full shortly. For now, I'll continue to make use of this notion without attempting to analyze it, though I hope that my employment of the concept will assist in its explication.

The question of possible worlds comes up immediately when one asks what exactly it means to be a possible person. A possible person is a person who exists in a possible world, presumably, in a great many possible worlds. But is there such a person as Caesar because there is a possible world containing Caesar, or is the reverse true? I believe the reverse is true, but for now, my question is: What is it for what is possible to become actual, for a possible person to become an actual person, i.e. to be born or conceived, or to die and exit the actual world? Is it for there to be traffic between possible worlds via some "Transworld Airlines"?[1] Luper, whom we encountered when discussing Feldman's "termination thesis," in his entry on "Death" in the *Stanford Encyclopedia of Philosophy* appears to believe the answer to the question of transworld traffic is yes.[2]

Well, where do you go when you're dead? As has already been pointed out, it's not to the grave. That's where your corpse goes, if it still exists. Perhaps, then, you go to heaven or to hell? Perhaps, but as indicated earlier in this study, I'm bracketing the question of whether human beings have immortal souls.[3] Is it, then, to another possible world? After

---

1. I borrow this term, with a twist, from "Transworld Heir Lines" (Kaplan 1979).

2. Luper 2014b.

3. By contrast, as indicated earlier, Plato in *The Phaedo* argues for the existence of the immortal soul. He speaks not of *the being* of Socrates (or the being, Socrates) but rather of *the existence* of Socrates's soul, and, at least for argumentative purposes, he does think of birth and death as "migration" or "travel" of a sort to and from "this" world," the actual physical universe. Since he believes the soul is immortal, however, there's no question for him of the soul's coming into and going out of existence as it travels between worlds. If, however, one were to speak not of the soul itself but rather of the embodiment of the soul, the situation is altered. In the dialogue, Socrates makes it clear that when he dies, the concrete embodiment of his soul to which his disciples have become attached will be gone, will have ceased to exist. And of course, what doesn't exist can't be buried. Which is why, asked how he should be buried, Socrates replies that whatever they choose to bury won't be *him*—that embodied self they are now addressing.

all, even if you no longer belong to the actual world, as a no-longer-actual-but-still-possible-person, you still exist in many possible worlds (if one accepts, contra David Lewis, the idea of transworld identity). Nothing, including death, can alter the fact that you are a possible person, someone who exists in many possible worlds. But that doesn't mean that when you die, you travel to another world. Yet Luper appears to believe that when you die, you do indeed embark on such a transworld journey. "[O]n Yourgrau's view," he says, "it seems entirely impossible for any individuals to live any longer than they actually do. Suppose that (say) Socrates might have lived an additional 10 years. Shouldn't it follow that over the course of the 10 years following his actual death Socrates was an object living outside of the actual world? Yet Yourgrau contends that no nonactual objects are alive."

What Luper has to say here needs to be taken seriously. It demands a response. He's one of the leading figures in the philosophy of death. Besides being the author of *The Philosophy of Death* (Luper 2009) and the editor of *The Cambridge Companion to Life and Death* (Luper 2014a), he has, as we've seen, been chosen to write the entry on "Death" for the *Stanford Encyclopedia of Philosophy*. In response, then, to Luper, I begin by recalling what I pointed out earlier in discussing his essay "Existence," that it should be clear that the view of mine that Luper's criticizing is that when you die, you cease to be *actually* alive. You don't cease being *possibly* alive—i.e. alive in some possible world. When I say that, in Luper's words, "no nonactual objects are alive," what I mean is that "nonactual objects aren't *actually* alive"—not, "nonactual objects aren't *possibly* alive, i.e. alive *in some possible world*." Nonactual objects aren't up to anything in the actual world. A nonactual king will never occupy an actual palace. As Derek Parfit says in Appendix J, "On What There Is":[4] "Nothing that isn't actual could be in an *actual* palace" (2011, 274). To say, then, that Socrates might have lived an additional ten years is to say that in some possible world, Socrates lives ten more years than he lived in the actual world. *Pace* Luper, there's nothing in my view that implies the contrary.

Note, further, that Luper says that if Socrates could have lived for ten more years than he actually did, "over the course of the 10 years following his actual death Socrates was an object living outside the actual world." Unless he simply expressed himself poorly,[5] his words imply that when one dies and (as one says) "takes leave of this world," one travels to some other possible world(s), in which one "continues" to live. I hope that's not what he meant, since such a view makes no sense. There is, of course, no travel between possible worlds, no Transworld Airlines. What's true, rather, is that Socrates exists in many possible worlds. His life and death in the actual world do not in the least affect this fact (about, as it were, "modal space" or the nature of modal reality, as a whole). Otherwise put, death erases your existence in the actual world; it doesn't touch your existence in other possible worlds. There was no parade held for Socrates

---

4. Thanks to Eli Hirsch for drawing my attention to this appendix.

5. Unless, that is, all he meant to say was that there are possible worlds in which Socrates lives for ten more years than he lived in the actual world. "Over the course of the ten years following his actual death Socrates was an object living outside the actual world," however, which is what Luper actually says, sounds an awful lot like "over the course of the ten years following Sam's release from prison, he was a model citizen living in the outskirts of Miami." When you die, you don't quit this world and take up residence someplace else, as Sam did when he moved to Miami.

when, on leaving our world, he showed up in another, ready for another ten good years. Similarly, before he entered this world, Socrates was not "waiting in the existential wings" (van Inwagen) or "drifting about" in this world (Thomson), or cooling his heels in some other possible world, anxious about his arrival here. Rather, Socrates could become actual, could be born, in virtue of the fact that, unlike Aphrodite, there is such person as Socrates, a possible person who, if conditions are right, can be actualized.

So much for Luper's first concern about my views about death and possible persons. His second worry is that, "together with the reasonable assumption that life is an essential attribute of persons, Yourgrau's view implies that it is impossible for any merely possible objects to be people. In that case we would have to reject Yourgrau's claim that dead and unborn people are real objects (who have the bad luck not to enjoy existence)." Luper's point is that "since Yourgrau contends that no nonactual objects are alive," it follows that no nonactual objects can be persons, since "life is an essential attribute of persons." Well, life is indeed an essential attribute of persons, as I've been insisting. But what does this mean? It means, as Aristotle said, that "for living things, it is living that is existing," from which it follows that for living things—like Socrates—not living, for example, being dead, means not existing. Not existing where? In the case of Socrates, in the actual world. The death of Socrates we're speaking of is not an event in some other possible world. It is an event in the *actual* world. Socrates no longer exists in the actual world for the simple reason that he's dead—i.e. *actually* dead. That, in Fine's terms, is a worldly fact. But from this fact nothing whatsoever follows about Socrates's existence in other possible worlds. His death "here" has no effect on his life "there."

And since Socrates, we're assuming, is essentially a living being, and, in particular, a person, in those possible worlds, at those times when he exists, he's alive and a person. Luper is thus entirely off the mark in claiming that "Yourgrau's view implies that it is impossible for any merely possible objects to be people."

Are we done with Luper? Far from it. "[I]n response to the second worry," he says,

> Yourgrau would deny that life is an essential attribute of persons. His view seems to be that Socrates is an object that, at one time, was a nonalive, nonactual person, that later came to be both alive and actual, that still later, died and yet remained a person, albeit one that is nonactual once again, and that continues to be a person now, long after Socrates's corpse has turned to dust. (Could such an object really be "a perfectly ordinary kind of concrete object"?) Instead of denying that life is essential to persons, Yourgrau could retreat to the position that some objects that are now merely possible are unlucky in that they will never be living persons. However, unless luck can hinge on the impossible, Yourgrau would have to justify the claim that some objects that at one time were nonalive nonpersons, later came to be live persons, and still later, the very same objects continued their careers—as dead nonpersons. If Yourgrau wanted to add that Socrates is such an object, he would have to make sense of how an object can be Socrates though it is not a person.

Luper's extended criticism, I confess, I find so muddled, I have trouble making sense of it. If we're talking about Socrates's career in the actual world, then, simply put, as "a perfectly ordinary kind of concrete object," he went from nonexistence, to existence, to nonexistence, similar to the career of, for example, New York's World Trade Center towers.

Since, to echo Aristotle yet again, for living things it is living that is existing, we can say that in the case of Socrates (as opposed to the World Trade towers) he went from being actually nonalive (i.e. prenatally nonexistent), to being actually alive, to being actually nonalive (i.e. dead). Whereas his *existential state*, thus, underwent a change during his career in the actual world, his *essence* did not. He remained, throughout, *a living-being*—something that cannot actually exist unless it's actually alive. He also remained (I'm assuming) a person—something that cannot exist unless it exhibits the traits of personhood. Since essence in this sense (i.e. essence*; cf. chap. III) is something that cannot be lost or gained, Socrates was *a person* before, during, and after life ("long after [his] corpse turned to dust"), though he *actually* exhibited the traits of personhood in the *actual* world only so long as he *actually* existed. He is now, as everyone knows, a dead person (not a dead nonperson)—someone who has forfeited his existence, but not his essence*.

So much for what birth and death mean when one talks of possible worlds. There remains, however, the question of how exactly things enter into and exit from our world. To modify the old joke about death and comedy, in general, dying is easy, being born is hard. There's nothing to it when it comes to exiting the actual world. If you're a person, all it takes is a razor blade[6] and the job is done. In fact, you don't need any equipment at all, as long as you have a lot of patience. While if it's your watch you'd like to exit this world, a few blows from a hammer is all the persuasion it takes.

---

6. A sad fact that so precious an object is so easy to dispatch. "The infinite which is in man," writes Simone Weil, "is at the mercy of a little piece of iron" (*Gravity and Grace* [1992], 75).

Entering this world, by contrast, is another matter entirely. We've already ruled out, in the case of persons, booking a seat on Transworld Airlines. We've dismissed, that is, the possibility of bringing someone into existence by traveling to another possible world where that person exists, grabbing her, then escorting her back to this world. How, then, does one do it?

The answer should be obvious. It all depends on the kind of being in question. As I said, if you want your priceless, golden, manual-wind Lange & Sohne wristwatch to exit this world, all you'll need is a few seconds alone with your watch and a hammer. By contrast, if you'd like to bring a watch like that into the world, you'll need to join a team of expert Lange craftspeople and have a lot of time on your hands. If we're talking about a priceless statue, it enters this world, it comes into existence, when you carve it out of a large piece of marble. Easy enough to destroy it, to cast it out of this world, but it takes a Michelangelo to create it, to bring it into the world. If it's a building, you build it. If we're talking painting, you'll need a paintbrush, some paint, and a piece of canvas. Want to bring a tree into this world? You'll need seed, soil, sunlight, and water. Human beings, thanks to Mother Nature, are especially easy, at least in the beginning phase. Typically, sexual intercourse will do the trick. And so on. In sum, just as you don't *enter* this world, you aren't born, by migrating *from* another world, you don't *exit* it, you don't die, by migrating *to* another world.

Still, this may seem a bit too quick, indeed, a bit too magical. At least part of the reason, I suspect, is that one doesn't usually consider the activity of creation *from an ontological point of view*, that is, as bringing a new individual into the world. The same may apply to the phenomenon

I alluded to earlier, people's reluctance to say, simply, that someone has ceased to exist. To be sure, as noted earlier, this assumes that in creation one does really bring into this world a new individual. Indeed, the reluctance to accept the cases I mentioned as genuine examples of this may cause one to become skeptical of the assumption that these cases really do involve *individuals*—skeptical, perhaps, of *the very idea* of an individual.[7]

Leonardo, you might feel compelled to say, didn't literally bring a new *individual* into the world when he painted the Mona Lisa. After all, you might think, what did he "*really*" do except arrange some paint into new patterns on a canvas, or to speak still more reductively, what did he really do but cause various paint molecules to occupy new positions? And so on. I'm doubtful such reductive strategies can be successful, but that's an argument for another day. I'm proceeding on the assumption that Leonardo did bring something new into the world, did create a new individual, when he painted the Mona Lisa,[8] and that your parents

7. Even if one retains the idea of an individual, one might become suspicious of the idea of the transworld identity of individuals, i.e. of what Kaplan calls "haecceitism." That would mean, however, committing oneself to the idea of "worldbound individuals," and adopting, perhaps, a "counterpart theory" like Lewis's. Few, however, have been willing to give up the idea that an individual, not just his or her "counterpart," might have had a different history than he or she actually had. When Marlon Brando's character in *On the Waterfront* said, "I could have been a contender," he didn't mean, "My counterpart could have been [or, rather, is] a contender."

8. There's a question, however, that concerns exactly which individual we're talking about here—the physical object, the painted canvas that hangs in the Louvre, or, if it's something different, the work of art that's been so admired for centuries. Though the Mona Lisa, in the latter sense, is certainly an individual, is that individual a type or a token? Peter

are also responsible for the existence of a new individual, namely, you. And when your parents brought something new into the world, they were, speaking ontologically, *actualizing the possible.* For although you were new to this

Strawson, in "Aesthetic Appraisal and Works of Art" (in *Freedom and Resentment* [1974]), argues persuasively that "[a]ll works of art, certainly, are individuals; but all are equally types" (184). He reasons as follows. "[It is] a mere contingent fact that we are, for all practical purposes, quite unable to make reproductions of pictures and statues which are completely indistinguishable, by direct sensory inspection, from the originals. If this practical limitation did not exist, then the originals of paintings and works of sculpture, like the original manuscripts of poems, would not as such have any but sentimental value" (183–84). The reason is that "there could not be two different works of art which were indistinguishable in all the respects relevant to their *aesthetic* appraisal. . . . [T]he *criterion of identity* of a work of art is the totality of features which are relevant to its aesthetic appraisal" (185).

A perfect copy of the Mona Lisa is indeed distinguishable from the original, even if not by the naked eye, in that it lacks a property the original has, namely, *having been painted by Leonardo.* (Indeed, the copy may not have been *painted* at all.) This distinguishing property, however, is not an *aesthetic* one. Walter Isaacson's new biography, *Leonardo da Vinci* (2017), concludes with an analysis of the Mona Lisa that makes clear why the painting deserves the great reputation it enjoys. Nowhere does Isaacson mention "painted by Leonardo" as one of the things that makes that work of art great, though it doubtless is one of the properties responsible for the enormous monetary value of the token of that painting that hangs in the Louvre.

Matthew Kieran, in *Revealing Art* (2005), rejects Strawson's view, but I find his reasoning unpersuasive. (I thank Anna Christina Ribeiro for referring me to this book.) "Painting," he says, "seems intrinsically particular, and no matter how good even the most painterly copy or forgery is, something will always be lacking" (13). What exactly will always be lacking? "The copy," he says, "may happen to give you exactly the same rewarding experience that the original gives . . . but it is none the less *a copy* of the original work rather than another version. . . . What this shows is that *the relations* in which a particular work stands make an essential difference to the nature of the work—and thus to how it should be treated"

world, your parents could only have actualized the possible person you are if *there already was* such a person to actualize. To repeat: (a) nothing becomes actual unless previously possible, and (b) your parents are responsible for your actuality, not your possibility.

(15; emphases added). What Kieran fails to establish, however, is that these relations, such as being painted by Leonardo, are *aesthetically* relevant, are relevant, that is, to the beauty of the painting. Unless Kieran can demonstrate that, Strawson, in my view, wins the argument.

Interestingly, what follows if Strawson is right is that strictly speaking, Leonardo didn't really *create* the aesthetic object, the Mona Lisa. He created a token that revealed to us that type. Types are uncreated universals. The Mona Lisa, after all, consists of a particular arrangement of line and color. Leonardo didn't create those geometric shapes, nor those colors, nor the possibility of that particular arrangement on the canvas. Still, in the ordinary sense of "creative" (vs. "mechanical"), that was a most creative act. By contrast, your parents did do something strictly speaking creative in having you, but unlike the case of Leonardo, they should get no high marks for that "achievement." The relationship between sexual intercourse and the child that results is an "external" one. Good sex, sad to say, does not good babies make. By contrast, the relationship between artist and painting is an "internal" one. Good painting does good paintings make. Parents deserve high marks if the way they raise their child is especially good and especially creative. Paradoxically, simply having a child is one of the least impressive creative acts a couple can engage in.

VI

TAKING POSSIBLE

WORLDS SERIOUSLY

> This complex physical entity ('the dice', thought of as a single object) . . . after the throw [occupies an] actual state. But when we talk . . . of thirty-six possibilities, in no way do we need to posit that there are some thirty-five *other* entities, existent in some never-never land.
>
> —SAUL KRIPKE

HAVING DISCUSSED, IN TERMS OF possible worlds, where you go when you're dead and where you came from when you arrived, the time has finally come to address the question: just how seriously should one take talk of possible worlds? This is one of the most fraught questions in contemporary philosophy of logic and deserves a book of its own, but, as promised, I need to say something to pay off my debt to the reader. I note first, as the previous chapters have, I hope, made clear, that the question of the metaphysics of birth and death depends heavily on how to characterize talk of possible worlds and possible persons, though one would never guess this given the lack of attention paid to the issue of possible worlds by philosophers investigating the concept of death.

And the same is true in the other direction. Although in *Modal Logic as Metaphysics* (Williamson 2013), Timothy

Williamson advances metaphysical and logical ideas that are in many respects congenial with my own, and in particular, with my approach to the metaphysics of death, his own explicit discussion of death, in a book that runs to 429 pages of densely packed argument about the metaphysics of modality, is confined to two pages (28–29).

It behooves me, then, to say something, finally, about just how seriously one should take talk of possible worlds and possible persons. Historically, discussion of possible worlds occurred frequently among medieval philosophers, in particular, with reference to the ontological argument for the existence of God, the argument from the possibility of a perfect, necessary being like God, to its actuality.[1] Leibniz spoke of possible worlds—of God's creating the best of all possible worlds—and Wittgenstein, in the *Tractatus*, also, in some fashion, employed the notion. The idea entered the contemporary philosophical scene most recently when pioneering figures in the formalization of modal logic, in particular, Kripke, proposed a semantic interpretation of the formalizations in terms of the notion of possible worlds, in which one world, the actual one, was singled out for special attention. The basic idea is that a proposition is necessarily

---

1. Recently, formalizations of modal logic have reawakened interest in the argument. Gödel himself tried his hand at it, realizing, as did Leibniz, that the first step was the crucial one, to prove the possibility of a "perfect" being. J. H. Sobel (1987), however, discovered flaws in the details of Gödel's proof. C. A. Anderson (1990) and Anderson and M. Gettings (1996) attempted to make repairs, but the repairs diminished the epistemic force of the argument. Anderson and Gettings concluded that "the Gödel Ontological Arguer should simply admit that neither the possibility of God nor the truth of the axioms used to 'prove' that possibility are self-evident. And he might just maintain that the less evident axioms [are] assumption[s] which he adopts on grounds of mere plausibility" (171).

true iff true in all possible worlds, and possibly true iff true in some possible world. (I omit the complication Kripke introduced about the relative "accessibility" of one world to another.) A proposition free of modal operators is true iff true in the actual world.

An interpretation, however, is only useful if we understand it. What exactly are we talking about when we speak of possible worlds, and what makes the actual world so special? In Kripke's seminal essay "Semantical Considerations on Modal Logic" (1971), there is no indication that talk of possible worlds is not to be taken literally, nor that there is any asymmetry between the nature (as opposed to the existence) of the actual world and that of merely possible worlds. It's hardly surprising, then, that David Lewis, in *The Plurality of Worlds*, though he harbored serious misgivings about the distinction between abstract and concrete, argued that if there is a sense in which the actual world is something concrete, so must other possible worlds be, since he believed that "other worlds are of a kind with this world of ours" (1986, 81). But he took this *categorial symmetry*, this "modal realism," to extend to *existential symmetry*, proposing the principle of "the indexicality of actuality," the idea that being actual—actually existing—like being here, is an essentially relative notion. Just as no place is here, absolutely speaking, but only relative to itself, according to Lewis, no world is actual, absolutely speaking, but only relative to itself. In this he separated himself from Kripke, who singled out the actual world for special treatment.[2]

---

2. He also separated himself from Kripke's doctrine of transworld identity. If other possible worlds are as actual—as actually existent—as is the actual world, he believed, the same individual cannot exist in more than one possible world. Instead, individuals have "counterparts" in other worlds.

Modal realism, in Lewis's sense, however, has had few adherents, most rejecting both it and the principle of the indexicality of actuality. Salmon ridiculed it in "An Empire of Thin Air" (2008d), his review of Lewis, arguing that "Lewis confuses possibility with a kind of actuality" and that to hold that there "*might have been* tiny purple anthropologists" is not to commit oneself to "the existence of things that *are* authentic tiny purple anthropologists inhabiting authentic alternative universes" (124). Kripke himself warned against taking his talk of possible worlds too literally. In the preface to *Naming and Necessity*, he compared talk of possible worlds to "school exercises in probability" concerning the possible outcomes of throwing a pair of dice. If we speak of a pair of dice, he said, as "a complex physical entity," and consider the thirty-six possibilities that can result if the dice are thrown, then, if we throw the dice and produce the unique, actual situation in which they've landed, "in no way do we need to posit that there are some thirty-five *other* entities, existent in some never-never land, corresponding to the physical object before me [i.e. the dice, in the situation in which they actually landed]. . . . Nor need we ask whether these phantom entities are somehow composed of the same individual dice themselves but in 'another dimension'" (17). What Salmon calls "an empire of thin air" of the modal realist, Kripke, in a related context, characterizes as a kind of "never-never land."

As Kripke put it in the text of his book, "[T]he wrong way of looking at what a possible world is . . . [is to view it] as if it were a foreign country" (43), or "as [a] distant planet, like our own surroundings but somehow existing in a different dimension" (15). To avoid confusion, he said, "I recommend that 'possible state (or history) of the world', or 'counterfactual *situation*' might be better" (15; emphasis added).

Fair enough, though an innocent reader of "Semantical Considerations on Modal Logic" could be forgiven for naively assuming that when in that essay Kripke spoke of possible worlds and the actual world he meant to refer to *possible worlds* and *the actual world*. Indeed, Jon Barwise and John Perry, who are far from innocent readers, and who devoted an entire book to the notion of situations, stated in *Situations and Attitudes* (1983) that "Kripke's possible-world semantics for modal logic provided a tool that has been used to develop Frege's theory of meaning into a model theory of natural language. We [however] do not believe that there are *other possible worlds in the sense demanded of them by this theory*, only other ways this world of ours might have been and might be" (xiii; emphasis added). What Barwise and Perry propose, then, as an *alternative* to Kripke's reference to possible worlds in his seminal essay, is, according to Kripke, exactly what he himself means by possible worlds.

Still, we need to know exactly what a possible world is, including and especially the actual world. I pause for a moment to provide a clue, and more than a clue, that will indicate the direction in which I'll be going. I note that though, contra Lewis, I'm a "modal chauvinist"[3] vis-à-vis the actual world—as well as a "temporal chauvinist" vis-à-vis the present moment—I am, in a certain sense, also a "modal realist," though not in Lewis's sense, and I'm unhappy with Kripke and Salmon's rejection of modal realism. I believe that a

---

3. On modal chauvinism, see my essay "On Time and Actuality: The Dilemma of Privileged Position" (Yourgrau 1986), and *Gödel Meets Einstein* (Yourgrau 1999). For a background in the philosophy of indexicals or demonstratives, see the readings collected in *Demonstratives* (Yourgrau 1990) and also "Frege, Perry and Demonstratives" (Yourgrau 1982) and "Kripke's Frege" (Yourgrau 2012).

possible F is the same kind of entity as an actual F, with the only difference being that only the actual F (actually) exists. (Recall Kant's dictum, which, I argued, Salmon, like Ishiguro, was wrong to reject. One pays for one's sins.) Lewis is correct, then, that whatever possible worlds are, they're not different in kind from the actual world. If the actual world is (in some sense) concrete, so are merely possible worlds. (Assuming, naively, that what Kripke and Stalnaker call "the actual world" is a *world*. See below.)

It by no means follows, however, that merely possible worlds are, as Lewis contends, no less *actual* or *existent* than the actual world. I repeat: *concreteness must not be confused with actuality*. Whereas possible worlds for Kripke, in agreement with Robert Stalnaker,[4] are *abstract existents* (possible states of the world, i.e. properties), and for Lewis, *concrete existents* (like distant planets), on my view, in contrast to both Stalnaker and Lewis, possible worlds are **concretenonexistents**. As I see it, *pace* both Stalnaker and Lewis, possible worlds don't exist. They're nonexistent—i.e. nonexistent objects.[5] We're free, however, to quantify over them, as Kripke did in his seminal essay, in virtue of the fact

4. In the preface to *Naming and Necessity*, Kripke, after commenting that it was only "a terminological accident that 'possible worlds' rather than 'possible states', or 'histories' of the world . . . had been used," adds in a footnote: "Compare, e.g., the 'moderate realism' regarding possible worlds of Robert Stalnaker, 'Possible Worlds'" (1980, 20).

5. Interestingly, Graham Priest in "Meinongianism and the Philosophy of Mathematics" (2003) says that "Routley himself holds that worlds other than the actual are nonexistent objects. This strikes me as a very sensible view" (5, note 2). Priest and Routley are neo-Meinongians. We've reached the same conclusion by different routes. Note, by contrast, that on Stalnaker's approach possible worlds aren't possibly *worlds* (as Fine puts it [see text, below]), since a property isn't possibly a world, and properties

that (*pace* Quine) the existential quantifier expresses not existence, but being.

So what exactly is a possible world? Let's start with the actual world. "The world," says Wittgenstein in the *Tractatus*, "is everything that is the case. The world is the totality of facts, not of things.... The facts in logical space are the world" (1961, 1–1.13). And what exactly is a fact? A fact,[6] as I see it, is a situation, for example, the situation that I'm currently writing this book. It isn't a mere collection of objects, nor a collection of objects together with properties. It consists, rather, of objects and properties being "situated" in a particular way, in a particular *state*. But what kind of entity is a situation, in this sense, abstract or concrete? Concrete. As Barwise and Perry insist in *Situations and Attitudes*, "An abstract state of affairs or course of events is a set. It is not perceived, does not stand in causal relations to other abstract situations and does not occur in nature.... Real situations are not sets, but parts of reality" (57–58). If, then, as Christopher Menzel puts it in his entry "Possible Worlds" in *The Stanford Encyclopedia of Philosophy*, we keep enlarging the situation of my writing this book so that it includes not just myself and my properties and how they're situated here and now, but everything that exists, we get a *maximal situation*, the actual world. Things, however, might have been otherwise. There are other possible maximal situations, which differ from the actual maximal situation, the actual world, not

actually, not merely possibly, exist. Paradoxically, so-called "possible world theory," for Stalnaker and Kripke, turns out not to be about *possible worlds*!

6. Frege, however, and more recently Quine and Davidson, rejected the notion of a fact, but, as pointed out in chapter I, the argument against facts—made precise by Gödel and Alonzo Church—is flawed.

vis-à-vis concreteness, but rather vis-à-vis actuality. These are the merely possible worlds, possible maximal situations that might have, but have not actually, obtained.

By contrast, Kripke says in *Naming and Necessity* that talk of possible worlds is actually misleading. "I recommend," he comments, "that 'possible state (or history) of *the world*', or 'counterfactual situation' might be better" (15; emphasis added). He says, similarly, that " '[p]ossible worlds' are 'total ways *the world* might have been' or states or histories of the *entire* world" (18; first emphasis added). Shortly thereafter, he says that "[t]he 'actual world'—better, the actual state, or history of *the world*—should not be confused with the enormous scattered object that surrounds us" (19–20; emphasis added). And, as we've seen, in a footnote (20, note 19), he defers to the "moderate realism" of Robert Stalnaker in his classic essay "Possible Worlds" (1979). Stalnaker appears to accept Lewis's thesis that possible worlds are "ways things might have been," pointing out, however, that "[t]he way things are is a property or state of *the world*, not *the world* itself" (emphasis added), and that "if properties can exist uninstantiated, then the way *the world is* could exist even if a world that is that way did not" (228).

This all begs the question, what exactly does the definite description "the world" refer to in these quotations from Kripke and Stalnaker? If a possible world is a way the world can be, does that mean, paradoxically, that the actual world is *the way* the world is? In a sense yes, says Stalnaker: "Compare: the way the world is is the world" (228). But that's not good enough. "The statement that the world is the way it is," says Stalnaker, "is true in a sense, but not when read as an identity statement" (228). Very well, but that still doesn't tell us what *the world itself* is, if not taken to be *the way* the world is. It's not as if there is just this property, the way the world is. This property is actually *instantiated*. Instantiated *by what*? The world, say Stalnaker and Kripke, but without telling us, explicitly, what this thing, the world, *is*. Could it be what Kripke calls "the enormous scattered object that surrounds us"—i.e. presumably, the physical universe, the cosmos, a large, scattered physical object? It can't be if we accept Wittgenstein's view that "the world is all that is the case," or the view of Barwise and Perry that the world is a maximal situation or state of affairs. It can't be, it would seem, if we believe cosmologists that the cosmos, the physical universe, is expanding. If it's expanding, which stage of the expansion is supposed to be the object that instantiates the property, the actual world (understood as the actual state of the world)? Or is it that the actual world is itself "expanding" or changing? Kripke and Stalnaker don't say.

Perhaps some light can be shown on this if we consult Christopher Hughes, who, in *Kripke: Names, Necessity and Identity* (2004, 135–37), addresses these issues head on. He argues that Kripke and Stalnaker can easily straighten all this out once they've clarified what exactly is meant by the terms "possible worlds," "the actual world," and "the world." According to Hughes, "[I]f a theologian says that there are many possible worlds that God could have created *ex nihilo*, in that context a possible world is not a different kind of thing from a (genuine) world. It is not an abstract entity—a (maximal) way things might have been. It is a universe, or something very like a universe. But possible worlds in what might be called *the theologian's sense* . . . are not possible worlds in *the modal logician's sense*. After all, for each of the many possible worlds that God might have created, there are many (maximal) ways that the world could have been"

(136–37; emphases added). If I understand Hughes correctly, the world in "the theologian's sense"—which is close to the ordinary, naive sense, as opposed to the Pickwickian sense of "a way the world can be"—is simply the cosmos, the physical universe, Kripke's "large scattered object surrounding us."

If he's right, it would have been nice if either Kripke or Stalnaker had explicitly stated this. Yet nowhere in the text of *Naming and Necessity* or in the new preface does Kripke mention possible worlds in the theologian's sense as one legitimate conception, to be contrasted with another legitimate conception that is employed in the semantics of modal logic,[7] even though, especially in the preface, he's at pains to explain away misconceptions about the nature and reality of possible worlds. On the contrary, he ridicules, in effect, the theological conception of alternative possible worlds, a form of modal realism,[8] as belief in never-never land.

7. Note that John Burgess, in *Saul Kripke: Puzzles and Mysteries* (2013), in his account of Kripke's conception of possible worlds, fails to mention these two distinct, but supposedly equally legitimate, conceptions. On the contrary, he stresses that "Kripke recognizes that 'possible world' talk may be misleading . . . [and] has encouraged thinking of counterfactual situations, ways the world isn't but might have been, as if they were 'possible worlds' in the sense of remote planets . . . [which means] [t]hinking of them as things or places seen through some sort of telescope" (49). What Hughes calls possible worlds in the theologian's sense are, of course, *not* like planets seen through some sort of telescope, which seems, however, to be *the only alternative* to the conception of possible worlds as possible states of "the world" entertained by Kripke or by Burgess, in his account of Kripke.

8. Though, of course, Lewis's modal realism also includes the proposition that other possible worlds are no less *actual* than is the actual world, which Kripke is right to reject.

Given this, it's unsurprising that Fine, like me, does not read Stalnaker's words the way Hughes does. "Stalnaker (1976, 230) and Plantinga (1974, 44)," writes Fine, "have suggested that we might think of a possible world as a way the world might have been. But *a possible world is possibly the world*, just as *a possible person is possibly a person*, yet no way the world might have been is possibly the world, just as no way I might have been is possibly me" (2004, 216; emphasis added). Compare: it would be perverse if Kripke and Stalnaker were to claim that possible people are simply possible states of "the people" (who exist), just as possible worlds are merely possible states of "the world" (that exists). In Kripke's case, not just perverse but inconsistent, since, as we saw earlier, Kripke (1971, 65) states that "in worlds other than the real one, some actually existing individuals may be absent, while *new individuals* . . . may appear." Clearly, by "new individuals" he doesn't mean "new states of 'the individuals' (that happen to actually exist)."

Perhaps I'm missing something, but nowhere do I see evidence from Kripke that he acknowledges the legitimacy of the theologian's sense of a possible world, which, according to Hughes, "is not a different kind of thing from a (genuine) world," i.e. is not a different kind of thing from "the world," a *concrete* object, "the enormous scattered object that surrounds us," as Kripke describes it. On the contrary, although according to Salmon, Kripke has at least three different conceptions of what a possible world is, according to all three, a possible world is an *abstract* object. "Nowadays," Salmon writes, philosophers . . . commonly regard possible worlds as *abstract entities* of a certain sort . . . maximal situations that might have obtained (Saul Kripke), maximal histories the cosmos might have had (Kripke), total states

the cosmos might have been in (Kripke, Robert Stalnaker)"
("Existence," 2008b, 31; emphasis added)

Further, one would have thought that modal logic, concerned not only with what's actual but with all that's possible,
would enjoy the greatest scope a theory could have. After
all, unlike other theories, it's not confined to what's actually
the case. Yet, if Hughes's interpretation is correct, Kripke's
possible-world semantics for modal logic resembles the state
of cosmology before Edwin Hubble and his telescope. You'll
recall that when Hubble pointed his telescope at the heavens,
he discovered that the extent of the cosmos as it was known
then—basically, the Milky Way—is but a tiny sliver of the
actual size of the universe. Possible world semantics, in turn,
on Hughes's interpretation, would appear to concern itself
with only a tiny corner of "modal space." Instead of ranging
over all things possible, modal logic would range over only
all that's possible concerning our own, particular universe.

As noted above, it would be as if a proposed "possible
persons" theory were to turn out to concern itself only with
possible states of the people who happen to actually exist.
The possible world interpretation of modal logic would be
silent on all the other indefinitely many universes "in the
theologian's sense," each with indefinitely many "ways they
could be." The price of making sense of Kripke's theory would
thus be to shrink its range of application to a nearly infinites-
imal sliver of modal space, compared to which the confine-
ment of pre-Hubble cosmology to the Milky Way would be
negligible.

A further problem is that even if Hughes were right
about Kripke's and Stalnaker's view about the referent of "the
world" and about Kripke's possible world semantics being
only about possible states of the physical universe, it would

remain that Kripke has posed no constraints on how far these possible states of the physical universe could differ from the actual state of the universe, and still be taken to concern our world, "the world." Would it still, for example, be our physical universe if it contained completely different laws of nature, had a radically different number of dimensions, contained radically different matter and energy, was inhabited by all new individuals, etc.? And if there are no constraints, why take the possible worlds in the theologian's sense to be different worlds from "the world" (i.e. why believe that other worlds are possible)?

And yet how could it be that there are no constraints on how different our universe could be without ceasing to be our universe, whereas for people, there are such constraints? Kripke, after all, advanced the thesis of the necessity of origin, which implies, he claimed, that no one in another possible world could be Socrates who didn't possess the property of having Socrates's parents. Kripke, that is, distinguished, à la Aristotle, between necessary and accidental properties. Does that distinction apply to people , but not to worlds containing people ?

And there would still be the question of the ontological status of these possible universes "in the theologian's sense." Unlike the possible universes of the modal logician, which, by Stalnaker's account, qua abstract objects, actually *exist*, the question of the ontological status of possible worlds considered as mere possibilia, as nonexistents, would need to be resolved. Here, I would answer by saying that the theologian's possible worlds should be taken seriously; like merely possible people, though nonexistent, they don't lack *being*. Salmon and Kripke would be wise to moderate their complaints against Lewis's "empire of thin air," the "never-never land" of the modal realist, since even if the modal realism of Hughes's theologian is not the same as Lewis's, it remains a form of modal realism all the same, one that accepts the view that Lewis put forward that possible worlds are of the same kind as the actual world—concrete, if that's what the actual world is, though, *pace* Lewis, unlike the actual world, *concrete and nonexistent.*

Even if one accepts Hughes's interpretation of Kripke and Stalnaker and acknowledges my distinction between being and existence, however, there remain unresolved issues concerning possible world theory. For one, there are facts or situations that it is difficult to "locate" in modal space. Is the fact, for example, that some Socrates-less possible world lacks Socrates, a fact contained in that possible world, or rather a fact not *in* but only *about* that world, as some would say? If the latter, in what world *does* that fact exist?[9] Here, as is so often the case, there's a parallel between questions in modal logic and questions in tense logic. It was Aristotle, the originator of both temporal and modal logic, who first raised a related problem of tense logic concerning the "location" of certain temporal facts, a problem that, arguably, is still with us, the so-called problem of future contingents. If a prediction of what will happen in the "open future" turns out, in the future, to be right, does that mean that already in the past, when the prediction was made, it was true then—implying, seemingly, that the "open" future was not after all so open?[10]

9. Kripke confronts this question in "Second General Discussion Session" (1974b) and says he's of two minds about how to answer it. See "Kripke's Moses" (Yourgrau 2013).

10. Though some believe this problem has been solved using concepts from so-called "branching tense logic," I disagree. See *Gödel Meets*

And there are other facts that are similarly elusive. This world—our world, the real world—is actual. That is to say, it *happens* to be actual, though it might not have been. I'm referring to *the contingency of actuality*. Where should we locate this fact? It can't be a fact within the actual world, since, as Lewis emphasized, every possible world is actual relative to itself. Every possible world, so to speak, "from within," takes itself to be actual, but that doesn't make it actual from an absolute point of view. Analogously, every proposition, so to speak, "takes itself to be true," but that doesn't make it true. As Frege pointed out, if I say, "I'm telling you the truth," it doesn't follow that I'm telling you the truth. The truth (more precisely, the truth-value) of a proposition is not, as it were, a *constituent* of a proposition. Frege calls it the *referent* of a proposition or thought.

Where, then, as we were just asking, is the fact that our world happens to be the actual world located, if not in our world itself? Would it help to postulate a "superworld," *s*, in which it's a fact that our world, the actual world, *a*, obtains? Unfortunately, no, since the contingency of the actuality of world *a* would need to be represented by the contingency, in turn, of superworld *s*, which itself doesn't necessarily, but merely happens to, obtain. We would need to postulate, in turn, a "supersuperworld," *S*, in which it's a fact that superworld *s* obtains, and so on, leading to an infinite regress

Einstein (1999, 126–40), where I cast doubt on a sophisticated attempt by Richmond Thomason (1970), "Indeterminist Time and Truth-Value Gaps," to demonstrate that we can have future truth without future necessity. The problem was an acute one for medieval philosophers, given the assumption of God's omniscience. See William Ockham (1983), *Predestination, God's Foreknowledge, and Future Contingents*.

of "superworlds."[11] On the other hand, the actuality of the actual world can't be a transcendental fact in Fine's sense, i.e. part of what constitutes the very fabric of modal space, since the actuality of the actual world is, as I've insisted, a contingent fact, whereas the fabric of modal space is something necessary and unalterable. So, a dilemma.

All this assumes, of course, that the actual world is, indeed, ontologically privileged. In his seminal paper "Semantical Considerations on Modal Logic," Kripke, as we saw, assumes this without argument. He simply introduces a model structure as "an ordered triple (G, K, R) where K is a set, R is a reflexive relation on K, and $G \varepsilon K$. Intuitively, we look at matters thus: K is the set of all 'possible worlds'; G is the 'real world'"[12] (emphasis added). By contrast, Lewis, as we've discussed, challenged the singling out of one possible world on the basis of his doctrine of the indexicality of actuality. That controversial doctrine only applies, however, if one already accepts ontological parity among possible worlds. Stalnaker, however, in "Possible Worlds" (1979), argued against parity: "The thesis that there is no room in reality for things other than the real world is not, like solipsism, based on a restrictive theory of what there is room for in reality, but rather on the metaphysically neutral belief that 'the actual world' is just another name for *reality*" (229) (emphasis added).

It's not clear, however, in what sense this is a "metaphysically neutral belief." After all, as we just saw, Kripke

11. See "On Time and Actuality: The Dilemma of Privileged Position" (Yourgrau 1986, 411) and Olla Solomyak, "Actuality and the Amodal Perspective" (2013, 22, note 12).

12. Kripke 1977, 64.

introduced as part of a model for modal logic a set of all possible worlds, of which the actual world was simply one, singled out as somehow special. Doesn't *reality*, on that view, include not just that one world but rather *all the worlds in that set*? Not to mention the fact just discussed of the contingency of the actuality of the actual world, which is not contained in the actual world itself. Is that fact, absent from the actual world, not part of reality? And how about the transcendental facts that Fine speaks of that are part of the very framework of possible worlds? Are they not part of reality?

As for the question of the parity of possible worlds, there seems to be a trade-off, apparent already in Kripke's presentation of his model, between acknowledging the other possible worlds and simply declaring one of them to be special, vs. recognizing only the actual world and then trying to find a way, somehow, to acknowledge the other possible worlds without "recognizing" them. Solomyak, in "Actuality and the Amodal Perspective" (2013), addresses this trade-off. She speaks of two fundamental intuitions: "**M1**: The actual state of affairs is but one of many ways the world *could have been*, and **M2**: What is actually the case is absolutely the case, above all other possibilities" (16). Both intuitions, she argues, are legitimate, but unfortunately, they're inconsistent with each other. They represent "two metaphysically privileged perspectives—two equally fundamental senses of what it is to be *real*. One sense of *reality*, or *way of being*, is the *modal* sense, which we can call *being*$_m$. In the modal sense, the actual world is *all there is*$_m$, and what is *actually* the case is an *absolute*$_m$ fact of reality. The second sense of what it means to be real is the *amodal* sense, which we can call *being*$_{am}$. From the amodal perspective, all possible states of affairs are metaphysically on a par, i.e. all possibilities

are_{am}. The $absolute_{am}$ facts of reality are amodal facts, which are blind to actuality" (34). As for the relationship between these two senses of what is real, "[W]hat is the case in the modal sense cannot be thought of as a mere restriction of what is the case amodally—rather, what is $real_m$ exists in a fundamentally different way than what is $real_{am}$" (34). The conclusion she draws is as follows: "There simply is no general sense of what it means to be real that encompasses *both* of these perspectives, or ways of being. . . . We don't express M1 and M2 as conflicting intuitions we aren't sure how to resolve, but rather as two complementary features of a single coherent position" (34–35) (emphasis added). Aware of the analogy between modality and tense, she argues for a similar approach to the question of the ontological privilege of the present moment over past and future times.

Solomyak, I believe, has offered a thought-provoking new perspective on the question of the actuality of the actual world, reminiscent of Neils Bohr's idea of complementarity in quantum mechanics. I'll respond to it briefly, though it deserves a comprehensive reply. There's definitely something right about it. One might think, in fact, that Solomyak's two senses of *being* are definitional equivalents of my distinction between being and existence. I don't think so, however. Ultimately, in maintaining that on her view there are "two equally fundamental senses of what it is to be *real*," Solomyak, is making yet another attempt—albeit a highly original one—to find a way around the paradox of nonexistence. For by "what it is to be *real*," Solomyak means, I take it, "what it is to *exist*," just as she holds that "[t]he modal realist is . . . ontologically committed to possible worlds as *genuinely existing* entities" (17; emphasis added), whereas on my version of modal realism, possible worlds are *nonexistent*, although they're not fictions but rather genuine *worlds* which possess not existence but being.

Further, unlike the distinction between being and existence, her distinction between two different senses of real implies that, in effect, one is *speaking two different languages*, or at least two different idiolects, when employing two distinct senses of the term "real." By contrast, I don't believe I'm employing two different idiolects when I speak of being vs. existence. I'm reluctant, therefore, to give up my intuition that the nonexistent—including merely possible worlds and merely possible people —really are *nonexistent*. Kaplan, as mentioned earlier, comes close to the distinction between being and existence, but in speaking, as he does, of "the more attenuated being of the nonexistents" (1989, 608), he seems to suggest that nonexistents have some, albeit "attenuated," purchase on existence, whereas on my view, being is not, as it were, a "thinned out" version of existence, but rather what underlies both existence and nonexistence. Here I'm with Quine. I don't want to ruin the good old word "exist." I'm also with Gödel, who said that "the notion of existence is one of the primitive concepts with which we must begin as given. It is the clearest concept we have. Even 'all', as studied in predicate logic, is less clear, since we don't have an overview of the whole world."[13]

The distinction between being and existence may be real or it may be an illusion, but it's not a distinction between two forms of *existence*. I can't, therefore, entirely endorse Fine's approach to this question, though it comes very close to my own. "Philosophers," says Fine in "Necessity and

13. Hao Wang attributes this remark to Gödel in his last book, *A Logical Journey: From Gödel to Philosophy* (Wang 1996).

Non-existence," "have been wedded to the idea that existence should be explained in terms of the quantifier, of what I have called 'being'; for an object to exist is for it to be, i.e. for there to be something that the object is. But think of existence as a certain very general kind of status; to exist is to be some sort of existent. It is not then so clear that existence should be tied to being" (2005, 352). This accords with the way I see things. It's what Fine goes on to say that begins to put some distance between us: "It might be thought odd that we take there to be a sense of existence in which Socrates necessarily exists. But we should bear in mind that this is an unworldly or transcendental form of existence; there is no worldly way in which Socrates has to be if he is to exist. We might think of existence in this sense as the invariable concomitant of any object being what it is" (353). To my mind, attributing not just existence but necessary existence to Socrates, even if it be only existence in the "unworldly or transcendental" sense, fails to make a clean break between existence and being, and thus, once again, fails to confront, head-on, the paradox of nonexistence. As will be seen later, Fine's approach resembles that of Timothy Williamson in "Necessary Existents" (2002), according to which Socrates necessarily exists in a special "logical" sense of existence. Where I speak of *nonexistence*, Fine and Williamson speak of *necessary existence*, albeit existence of a special kind.

In sum, I'm reluctant, in spite of having some sympathy for Solomyak's approach, to abandon my modal chauvinism, and so in the end I think Kripke was right to single out one possible world as special, even though I'm not convinced by Stalnaker's defense of this position. I don't have a better argument to offer for modal chauvinism, sorry to say, just an intuition I'm reluctant to give up, but an intuition backed up by the idea of the distinction between existence and being, which I'm also reluctant to abandon.[14] I'm also hesitant to give up temporal chauvinism, often called presentism. Yet presentism appears to conflict with contemporary physics, in particular, with Einstein's relativity. Doesn't this suggest that presentism is false? Should I simply accept the fact that by, in effect, merging time with space,[15] Einstein, among his other great achievements, should be credited with defeating death itself, by separating it from nonexistence?

14. Solomyak, however, also cites intuitions she's reluctant to abandon. Won't a battle like this between competing intuitions result in a standstill, suggesting that this is a flawed methodology? No. I think such a suggestion would be misguided. As Kripke said in *Naming and Necessity*, "[S]ome philosophers think that something's having intuitive content is very inconclusive evidence in favor of it. I think it is very heavy evidence in favor of anything, myself. I really don't know, in a way, what more conclusive evidence one can have about anything, ultimately speaking" (42). When intuitions compete, the battle between them must be fought. Some fights can't be avoided.

15. As to what exactly it could mean to merge time with space, and whether Einstein, with help from Minkowski, accomplished this feat, see "When Time Turned into Space" (Yourgrau 2014).

VII

TIME AND EXISTENCE

> The concept of existence cannot be relativized without
> destroying its meaning completely.
>
> —KURT GÖDEL

I'VE BEEN ASSUMING, TOGETHER WITH the vast majority of philosophers discussing the metaphysics of death,
that death means nonexistence. When you die, you cease to
exist. That assumption is based on the premise that the dead
are in the past, and that what's confined to the past doesn't
exist. Otherwise put, *what's past has passed*. Only what's happening now, in the present, is really happening. These days,
that goes by the name of presentism[1]. I've called it temporal
chauvinism, to bring out more clearly an analogy with what
I've been calling modal chauvinism. In the one account, *the
present moment* occupies a privileged position, ontologically
speaking, in the other, *the actual world* occupies a privileged
position. (Interestingly, there's great disagreement over temporal chauvinism, whereas most philosophers, I believe,
are modal chauvinists.) It's tempting to complete the verbal
analogy and speak in turn of actualism, though what usually
goes by that name is not quite the same thing as what I'm
calling modal chauvinism, since those who call themselves

1. There are in fact a variety of versions of presentism, which there's no
need to go into here.

actualists are reluctant, unlike myself, to describe themselves as modal realists.

Einstein enters the picture vis-à-vis temporal chauvinism insofar as special relativity appears to reject the idea that what's past has passed (from existence). Thus, in a much-quoted letter to his friend Michele Besso's widow about her late husband, Einstein wrote that "in quitting this strange world he has once again preceded me by a little. That doesn't mean anything. For those of us who believe in physics, this separation between past, present, and future is only an illusion, however tenuous."[2]

That would appear to settle the matter, at least as to what Einstein's view was of a privileged position in time. The matter, however, isn't quite so simple. Rudolf Carnap remarks in his "Intellectual Autobiography,"[3] "Once Einstein said that the experience of the Now means something special for man, something essentially different from the past and the future, but that this important difference does not and cannot occur within physics" (37–38). Thus Einstein's informal comments about the nature of time are inconclusive. The real question is what his physics, his theory of relativity, tells us. Before I get into that, however, I note that what we're now discussing, the question of time and existence, is, once again, something strangely ignored by most philosophers of death, with

2. Bernstein 1991, 165.

3. In P. A. Schilpp, ed., *The Philosophy of Rudolph Carnap* (Carnap 1963). The response by Carnap, one of the leading members of the Vienna Circle of logical positivists, is noteworthy: "But I definitely had the impression that Einstein's thinking on this point involved a lack of distinction between experience and knowledge."

a few exceptions.[4] Once again, the left hand doesn't know (or doesn't care) what the right hand is doing.

To get an idea of what the formal or mathematical theory of four-dimensional Einstein-Minkowski space-time implies about the *informal* or *intuitive* concept of time we need to have some understanding of both concepts. There's been a tendency, however, to bypass or minimize the intuitive notion, on the assumption that since the formal theory is now firmly established, there's no need to revisit the dark times when all we had were our informal intuitions. A perfect example of this tendency is what the noted philosopher of science Hilary Putnam wrote in "Time and Physical Geometry":[5] "Indeed, I do not believe that there are any longer any philosophical problems about Time: there is only the physical problem of determining the exact physical geometry of the four-dimensional continuum we inhabit" (205).

Gödel, by contrast, in his writings on Einstein, his close friend and colleague at the Institute for Advanced Study, was exceptionally clear about the need to understand the

4. Silverstein (1993), who has explicitly discussed (and rejected) presentism, is a notable exception. More recently, Connolly (2011) has explicitly discussed (and defended) presentism. For the most part, however, discussion of time among philosophers of death has concentrated on our how attitudes toward present, past, and future harms differ. That there's a hot debate going on among philosophers of space and time, and some physicists, as to what relativity has to say about the relationship of time to existence has apparently escaped the notice, or the interest, of most philosophers studying death.

5. In Putnam 1979. In fairness to Putnam, when Mark van Atten informed him that in a recent book I had taken him to task for that remark, his response was that he no longer held that view. Contrast Putnam's remark (1979) with what Kurt Gödel said to Hao Wang, that in a sense time is *the* philosophical problem.

relationship between the formal and the intuitive conceptions of time.[6] If one knows Gödel's work, that should come as no surprise. Hao Wang, one of his closest associates in his final years, described Gödel's investigations as a "dialectic of the formal and the intuitive." Indeed, one should speak, I believe, of the Gödel Program (by analogy with the Hilbert Program of mathematical formalism): *the attempt to establish, by formal methods, the limits of formal methods in capturing intuitive concepts.* Gödel himself saw his famous incompleteness theorem in mathematical logic in that light—as establishing, formally, the inability of a formal (*proof*) system (in the strict logical sense) of suitable strength, assuming it's consistent, to capture the intuitive concept of arithmetic *truth*—though too often these days, there's been a tendency to regard the theorem in a purely formal or syntactic light.

6. In particular, in his philosophical essay "A Note on the Relationship between Relativity Theory and Idealistic Philosophy" (1949), reprinted in Yourgrau 1990. He published separately two formal contributions to general relativity in which he constructed surprising new cosmological world models, in some of which, provably, there exist closed time-like world lines, i.e. time travel. If you can travel to the *past*, however, Gödel argued, time hasn't really *passed*, and so it must be merely ideal. (See Yourgrau 1999, *Gödel Meets Einstein*, and 2006, *A World without Time*.) Of these two essays, the cosmologist, G. F. R. Ellis, coauthor with Stephen Hawking of *The Large Scale Structure of Space-Time* (Hawking and Ellis 1973), wrote that "together they stimulated examination of themes that were fundamental in the development of the Hawking-Penrose singularity theorems" (Ellis 1996, 34). By contrast, John Stachel (2007) has written that "[t]o use [as Gödel did] the existence of a class of models with closed time-like world lines as an argument against the concept of time, without a shred of evidence that such models apply to any physical phenomena, is an example of that fetishism of mathematics to which some Platonists are prone" (867–68). (Gödel, of course, was well known for being a mathematical Platonist. He shared, as well, Plato's suspicions about the ultimate reality of time.)

As Gödel, however, wrote to Wang,[7] "[F]ormalists [like Hilbert] considered formal demonstrability to be an analysis of the concept of mathematical truth and, therefore, were not in a position to *distinguish* the two" (10). The same, arguably, mutatis mutandis, could be said of formally inclined philosophers and physicists and the concept of time.

Time in the intuitive sense Gödel characterized as "Kantian," "pre-relativistic," "what everyone understood by time before relativity."[8] The "objective lapse of time," he said, which seems to be "directly experienced," "involves a change in the existing."[9] Intuitive time is something "whose essence is that only the present really exists." With this characterization clearly in mind, he put forward a succinct argument that time in the intuitive sense is inconsistent with Einstein's (special) theory of relativity: "The existence of an objective lapse of time . . . means (or, at least, is equivalent to the fact) that reality consists of an infinity of layers of the 'now' which come into existence successively. But if simultaneity is something relative [according to special relativity], reality cannot

---

7. Quoted in Wang 1974.

8. In the literature, time in the intuitive sense is often identified with what J. M. E. McTaggart called the A-series, the temporal flux of "the now," the present: what was future becomes present, and then past. The B-series, by contrast, characterizes the nonchanging temporal order of events in terms of before and after, earlier and later. Thus, my writing this book is something that's happening now, but will soon (I hope) change into an event in the past. By contrast, that World War I occurred before World War II is a fact that will never change; it is "fixed." The B-series, one might say, is uniquely characterized by its geometry. According to McTaggart, the reality of time requires the reality of both the A-series and the B-series, which he thought was impossible. He concluded that time is not real but ideal.

9. Otherwise put, if time and change are real, "Reality grows by the accretion of facts," as Richard Jeffrey put it ("Coming True," Jeffrey 1980, 253).

be split up into such layers in an objectively determined way. Each observer has his own set of 'nows,' and none of these various systems of layers can claim the prerogative of representing the objective lapse of time" (1990, 262).

Einstein himself put the matter very similarly:[10] "Since there exist in this four-dimensional structure... [Minkowski space] ... no longer any sections which represent 'now' objectively, the concepts of happening and becoming are indeed not completely suspended, but yet complicated. It appears therefore more natural to think of physical reality as a four-dimensional existence, instead of, as hitherto, the *evolution* of a three-dimensional existence. . . . This rigid four-dimensional space of the special theory of relativity is to some extent the four-dimensional analogue of H.A. Lorentz's rigid three-dimensional aether" (150–51). The one crucial distinction between this statement and what Gödel wrote is Einstein's saying that in special relativity the concept of *becoming* isn't completely suspended, but only "complicated." It's hard to understand, however, how *becoming* or *change* persists in relativity theory in any sense, including a "complicated" one, if as Einstein himself points out, *evolution* has been eliminated, to be replaced by a *rigid* four-dimensional *space*. Can one make sense of a rigid nonevolving space *becoming*?[11] It's no accident that Karl Popper reported that in

10. *Relativity: The Special and General Theory* (Einstein 1961).

11. Quine (1987) disagrees. "When time is thus viewed [in relativity theory]," he says, "an enduring solid is seen as spreading out in four dimensions. . . . Change is not thereby repudiated in favor of an eternal static reality, as some have supposed. Change is still there, with its fresh surprises. . . . To speak of a body as changing is to say that its later stages differ from its earlier stages, just as its upper parts differ from its lower parts. Its later shape need be no more readily inferred from its earlier shape than its upper shape from its lower" (197). The parts, however, of Quine's

his conversations with Einstein, our old friend Parmenides made an appearance: "I tried to persuade him to give up his determinism, which amounts to the view that the world is a four-dimensional Parmenidean block universe in which change is a human illusion or very nearly so. (He agreed that this had been his view, and while I discussed it I called him 'Parmenides'.)"[12]

"enduring solid . . . seen as spreading out in four dimensions" do not come into existence successively. The solid is as "rigid" as what Einstein described as the "rigid four-dimensional space of the special theory of relativity." *What* exactly, then, is changing, according to Quine, *what* exactly is evolving over time, with regard to his enduring solid? The fact that one can't "readily infer" its later from its earlier shape has nothing to do with whether it's changing. One can't infer the exact "shape" of the distribution of later twin primes from the "shape" of the distribution of earlier ones, but that doesn't mean the prime numbers are *changing* over time.

What goes by the name of "time" in relativity theory, the fourth dimension of Einstein-Minkowski space-time, though it has a different mathematical signature from the other dimensions, behaves otherwise as if it were a fourth spatial dimension. Let's shrink Quine's example down one dimension, and consider a three-dimensional solid, say, a rocking horse. Its upper parts differ from its lower parts, and lengthwise, its tail differs from its mane. Its shape near its head need be no more readily inferred from its shape near its tail than its upper part from its lower. Does it follow that the various parts of the horse are *changing*?

Surprisingly, a mistake similar to Quine's is made even by noted physicists when they speak of an object *moving along* the path indicated in a Minkowski space-time diagram. This path, however, is not like a road along which one can travel. The path indicated in such a space-time diagram represents the journey itself. It's not a mere "spatial trace" of the journey. Not for nothing is Einstein's achievement in special relativity described as a geometrization of space and time, and in general relativity, of gravity. (For discussion of geometrization, see Yourgrau 1999, 12 and 43–45.) In his world models for general relativity, Gödel took advantage of Einstein's geometrizations and constructed *limit cases for the relativistic geometrization of time*. (See Yourgrau 1999, 12 – 15.)

12. Karl Popper, *The Open Universe: An Argument for Indeterminism* (1982, 2, note 2).

Einstein's comment reminds me of a typical reaction to the theory of relativity, namely, that it revolutionized our conception of time, or "complicated" it. Gödel had no time for such euphemisms. If by time we mean time in the intuitive sense, time that stands in categorial contrast to space, then the correct response to relativity is that far from *illuminating* time, by spatializing it,[13] Einstein *eliminated* it. A *space*, I suggest, in the most general sense, is *a manifold in which position conveys no ontological privilege*. Otherwise put, *where* you are in a space doesn't determine *whether* you are. If position in four-dimensional Einstein-Minkowski

13. That relativity spatializes time has been widely recognized. Quine, for example, speaks of the "spatializing of time" he recommends via the elimination, logically, of tenses as analogous to the treatment of time in relativity (Quine 1987, 197). Yet Einstein himself rejected this characterization of relativity, insisting "on the error of many expositions of Relativity which refer to 'the spatialization of time.' Time and space are fused in one and the same *continuum*, but this continuum is not isotropic, and the element of spatial distance and the element of duration remain *distinct in nature*, distinct even in the formula giving the square of the world interval of two infinitely near events" ("Comments on Meyerson's *La Deduction Relativiste*," in Čapek 1976, 366–67; second emphasis added).

I'm unhappy, however, with what Einstein says here. My reply in "When Time Turned into Space" (2014) is that "[i]t's hard to see . . . how exactly, in relativity, spatial distance and duration are 'distinct in nature.' They are distinguished, to be sure, in the formula for the interval, as Einstein insists, but this is in effect a *geometrical* distinction, not a representation of a categorial difference, à la Kant, of two different natures. In the formula of the Pythagorean theorem, for example, the hypotenuse is *distinguished* from the other two sides: the square of the hypotenuse is equal to *the sums of the squares* of the other two sides. Does this indicate that the hypotenuse is of a 'distinct nature' from the other two sides?" (206, note 3). The analogy with the Pythagorean theorem is actually quite close, since the formula for the space-time interval in relativity is in effect a generalization of the Pythagorean theorem. For a clear discussion of this, see the section "Spacetime Interval" here: https://en.wikipedia.org/wiki/Spacetime#Spacetime_interval.

space-time is ontologically neutral, it is thus a *space*—not, as Minkowski claimed, something that is neither a space nor a time. It represents a generalization of the concept of *space*, not, as is often claimed, a generalization of the concept of *time*. On this understanding, all space-time locations, in relativity, are equally existent, though of course, not all events are *simultaneous*.

Gödel goes on respond to an objection that is often made to the way he characterizes Einstein's theory:

> It may be objected that this argument only shows that the lapse of time is something relative, which does not exclude that it is something objective. . . . A relative lapse of time, however, if any meaning at all can be given to this phrase, would certainly be something entirely different from the lapse of time in the ordinary sense, which means a change in the existing. The concept of existence, however, cannot be relativized without destroying its meaning completely. It may furthermore be objected that the argument under consideration shows only that time lapses in different ways for different observers. . . . A lapse of time, however, which is not a lapse in some definite way seems to me as absurd as a colored object which has no definite colors." (262, note 5)[14]

14. Remember that Gödel is not rejecting Einstein's thesis of the relativity of simultaneity, nor relativistic time dilation, etc. He *accepts* the theory of relativity (at least in the present context; elsewhere, he suggests that physics took a wrong turn when it followed Newton [the empiricist], as opposed to Leibniz [the idealist]). What he denies is the thesis that this is a theory about *time*, in the intuitive sense. Rather, it's a theory about *space-time*, and the temporal dimension of space-time—the fourth dimension of Einstein-Minkowski space-time—Gödel is arguing, is not time in the intuitive sense, not even a *generalization* of it, as non-Euclidean space is a generalization of the concept of space.

Gödel's response, which to my ears sounds convincing, has failed to impress others. The noted Einstein scholar John Stachel, for one, is unimpressed by Gödel's reference to colors:[15] "[T]he perceived color of [an] object—and color is nothing but a perception—is a 'perspectival' effect, depending on the conditions of illumination of the object, the contrast with its surroundings, and the properties of the eyes and nervous system of the subject (ask a color-blind and a normal-sighted person whether all objects have a definite color!). So if one accepts Gödel's analogy, which we are under no obligation to do, it argues against rather than for his case" (866). Stachel is insisting that, *pace* Gödel, color is not an objective property of objects but only something dependent on the perspective of the observer. Gödel, however, is arguing against the claim that "the lapse of time is something *relative*, which does not exclude that it is something *objective*." He's saying that it's absurd to maintain that color—i.e. "the perceived color of an object"—is an *objective* property of an object ("in itself," as it were) and at the same time to hold that it is something that is merely *relative* to an observer's perspective. That would mean that something has a color, objectively speaking, but no *definite* color (since its color will differ relative to different perspectives). Stachel's insistence, against (he believes) Gödel, that color is *not* something objective, indicates that he has simply missed Gödel's point.

Even if we modify Gödel's analogy, however, so that it presupposes Stachel's claim that in fact, color is something merely relative to an observer's point of view, it argues rather for than against Gödel's case. The lapse of time, Gödel is

---

15. John Stachel, "Review: *A World without Time: The Forgotten Legacy of Gödel and Einstein*" (2007).

saying, "means a change in the existing," but, unlike your color (we're supposing), your existence isn't a mere "perspectival effect," different for different observes. Unlike appearing one color to some and another color to others, you can't *exist* according to one observer, yet *fail to exist* according to another, where neither observer "can claim the prerogative of representing the objective lapse of time," hence, the prerogative of representing the objective state of your existence.

Consider yourself, dear reader. Presumably you think it's an objective fact that you exist. How naive. You're clearly ignorant of relativity theory. You don't appreciate the fact that your existence isn't something objective, something nonrelative. On the contrary, it's relative. It depends on how different observers in different reference frames observe you. Certainly from your own perspective, you exist. But according to special relativity, your perspective is in no sense privileged. It doesn't represent the objective situation vis-à-vis the status of your existence. Is this a paradox in special relativity? Only if time in special relativity is taken to represent time in the intuitive sense, so that a lapse of time means a change in existence. Gödel's point, however, was precisely that *there is no such thing as the objective lapse of time* in the special theory of relativity and, thus, *a change in existence*. His argument was a reductio ad absurdum.

Yet, surprisingly, Charles Parsons (a noted authority on Gödel), in discussing Gödel's writings on Einstein, rejects the *reductio*, asserting that existence *can* be relativized! "It seems to me," says Parsons,[16] "simply wrong to say that existence cannot be relative to anything. . . . For example 'The World

16. "Gödel and Philosophical Idealism" (Parsons 2010).

Trade Center exists' is true relative to the context of utterance of 2000, but not relative to such a context in 2002" (180). So Parsons, it would appear, isn't prepared to say, simply, that he exists. If you ask him straight out, "Parsons, do you exist?" he would reply, "Well, it all depends on the context. 'Parsons exists' is true relative to the context of 2018, but it isn't true relative to the context of 1718. Absent that relativization of context, I can't answer that question." To my ears, that sounds absurd. If asked if Lincoln exists, the answer, surely, is no, not: well, in 1861, the answer is yes; in 2018, the answer is no. Of course, I'm speaking here intuitively, the way people on the street speak. If asked what special relativity says, that's another question, as is the question of how to interpret special relativity.

Parsons, it seems, can't make sense of the concept of intuitive time (or at least, what Gödel means by intuitive time).[17] The force, therefore, of Gödel's attempt, as in his

---

17. Stachel seems to believe that Gödel is simply wrong about the nature of intuitive time. He thinks Gödel is mistaken in claiming to discover such a dramatic conflict between our prerelativistic intuitive concept of time and time as it appears in relativity. "[W]e all have some intuitive concept of time," he writes. "Does it embrace the concept of a unique cosmic or *global* time, marching forward in lock step throughout the entire universe? The only intuitive concept of time that *I* have is a purely local one, associated with my progress through the universe" (2007, 864). I suspect, however, that Stachel's intuitions may have been too strongly influenced by his studies of Einstein. Before Einstein came along, I seriously doubt that time in the intuitive sense would have been taken to be a purely local affair. Who would have felt compelled to deny that if it is 4:00 p.m. by your watch, it is the same time down the street? And who, even today, absent knowledge of relativity, thinks this question becomes meaningless if it turns out to be a really, really long street?

As for time being "purely local," remember that we're talking here of our prerelativistic intuitive notion of time, which, as Gödel says, involves the idea that time passes or flows. Can one make sense of a merely local

incompleteness theorem, to find out if the intuitive concept, in this case, of time, can be captured by the "formal" concept, here, relativity theory, is lost on him.[18] For Parsons,

passage of time? Compare: though in a different sense, rivers also flow. Can a river flow, but only locally? Moreover, as Gödel says, the objective lapse of time, intuitively, means a change in the existing. Can your existence be a merely *local* affair? Would this not involve the same paradoxes we noted above, about the idea of a merely *relative* existence? Recall, again, that Gödel is not denying that *what passes for time* in Einstein's theory is a local, relative affair. What's he's saying is that precisely *because* that is true of Einstein's theory, what passes for time for Einstein is not really *time* at all (intuitively speaking). That's why Gödel is a temporal idealist, though a space-time realist.

Indeed, Stachel believes not only that time in the intuitive sense is compatible with relativity, but that it is at the very heart of the theory. "[In] the relativistic concept of time," he writes, "*process* is primary and absolute, while its division into spatial states evolving over time is secondary" (emphasis added). Process, however, means change, and, as Gödel argued, change means change in the existing, whereas "the concept of existence cannot be relativized without destroying its meaning completely."

Yet Stachel is in good company. Howard Stein makes the very same mistake when he writes of "[t]he leading principle that connects this mathematical structure [of relativity] with the notions of 'process' and 'evolution' and justifies the use of our notion of 'becoming' in relativistic space-time" ("On Einstein-Minkowski Space-Time," Stein 1968, 16). Stein gives the game away when he adds that "in Einstein-Minkowski space-time an event's present is constituted by itself alone" (15). As Simon Saunders points out in "How Relativity Contradicts Presentism" (2002), "because for Stein, it is a *fairly obvious consequence* of relativity theory that an event's present is constituted by itself alone . . . *[o]bviously* the presentist's position is untenable, given special relativity" (286). Which, of course, was exactly Gödel's point. Saunders sums things up well: "[O]n the tenseless point of view the fundamental ontological reality is the whole of Minkowski space and everything in it. . . . On the tenseless view, all events are real" (288).

18. Also lost on Parsons, as it has been, it seems, on almost everyone, is the asymmetry between Gödel's assessment of his two "incompleteness" arguments. In the case of mathematical truth, it was (consistent) formal axiomatic systems that were proven incomplete by Gödel. By contrast, the

it seems, the basic idea behind presentism is nothing but a tautology. "[T]he essence of an objective lapse [for Gödel]," says Parsons, "is that 'only the present really exists'. That is certainly at best a contentious assumption: so-called 'presentism' is at best a disputed view in the philosophy of time. One could object: Yes, only the present really exists *now*" (2010, 180). Parsons's objection could with equal justice be aimed at myself, since I wrote in a previous study[19] that "I find it exceedingly difficult to give up my intuition that dead people do not exist. . . . I do not mean merely that the dead do not *now* exist; for objects in time, what does not exist now does not exist at all" (141). As a matter of fact, in "The Evil of Death Revisited,"[20] Silverstein does aim in my direction exactly the same objection Parsons made against Gödel. "What *more*," he asks, "does Yourgrau think is being asserted by 'x does exist at all' than is being asserted by 'x does not exist now'?" (128).

My response will be ad hominem. If what Parsons and Silverstein are saying contra presentism or temporal chauvinism were correct, it would apply with equal force against actualism or modal chauvinism, a view I suspect both of them endorse (if not actualism, at least modal chauvinism). As the most famous opponent of modal chauvinism, Lewis, might say, what more do Parsons and Silverstein think is

---

failure, as he saw it, of relativity theory to capture intuitive time led him to abandon intuitive time, not to declare relativity theory "incomplete." A good question, unanswered because unasked, is why Gödel drew opposite philosophical conclusions from his two formal "incompleteness" results.

19. "The Dead" (1993).

20. Silverstein 2000.

being asserted by 'Only the actual world *really* exists' than 'Only the actual world *actually* exists'?" If their response, à la Stalnaker, would be to say that theirs is not a metaphysically restrictive view, since "the actual world" is just another name for reality, I, in turn, would reply that that form of reasoning could equally well be employed by the presentist, since the presentist, too, could argue that "the present" is just another name for reality. I conclude that the attempt by Parsons and Silverstein to reduce presentism to a mere tautology fails (unless they're willing to apply the same reasoning to modal chauvinism).

As I see it, then, Gödel's argument that special relativity, as classically understood, is inconsistent with the reality of intuitive time, is convincing. If this were the end of the story, that would be the end of time. Death could no longer be seen as ushering in nonexistence. There being no "coming into existence" successively of times and no consequent "passing out of existence," past times, where the dead reside, could no longer be considered less existent than the present time, and the dead would be no more nonexistent than the living. But this is not the end of the story, not least because special relativity is not the end of the story even for the theory of relativity.[21] I'll go into this, presently, but first I need to draw

---

21. Of course, there's also the question of general relativity, where gravity is taken into account. Gödel has an argument that there, too, time turns out to be merely ideal, but it's a much more complicated, modal argument based on Gödel's mathematical construction of surprising new world models for general relativity, mentioned above, in some of which there exist closed time-like world lines in which "time travel" is possible. This isn't the place to go into that (highly controversial) argument, long neglected. I discuss it in detail in Yourgrau 1999 and 2006. Gödel's remarkable argument, I'm happy to say, is finally receiving at least some of the attention it deserves.

attention to how one philosopher of death whom we've already met, Silverstein, has indeed invoked Einstein to help explain the ontology of death, obviating the need to confront the paradox of nonexistence, and, it might appear, thereby avoiding my invocation of a distinction between being and existence.

In "The Evil of Death" (1993) and "The Evil of Death Revisited" (2000), Silverstein illustrates that if one accepts, as he does, the metaphysical implications of relativity theory, conventionally understood, or what is popularly known as four-dimensionalism, one need not confront the paradox of nonexistence. As he puts it, "[T]emporally distant events, including posthumous events, exist, though they do not exist *now*" (1993, 119). He endorses what Quine said (citing a typescript of a lecture), that "[t]he simplest way of putting all this mess [created by tenses] in order is by viewing people and other physical objects as deployed in four-dimensional space-time and all as *co-existing in an eternal and timeless sense of the word*" (1993, 111; emphasis added). In other words, on this approach, *where* you're located in the four-dimensional space-time continuum doesn't determine *whether* you are. All objects located *somewhere* in this continuum of space-time *coexist*, though not all exist in the same "place" in four-dimensional space-time, just as in prerelativity, where you're located in space has no effect on whether you exist. Thus, according to this way of seeing things, the dead exist no less than the living, although their *locations* in space-time differ. Nothing could be simpler.

And yet, curiously, having presented this approach, Silverstein resists this way of understanding it. "[T]he four-dimensional framework," he says in "The Evil of Death Revisited," "emphatically does *not* imply that a human being's existence itself is either atemporal or eternal, and thus emphatically does not 'deny that someone's death is the end of his existence'" (2000, 128). On the contrary, "The four-dimensional framework is just as compatible with the claim that a human being's existence has *temporal boundaries*" (128; emphasis added). And yet again, "On the four-dimensional framework, as on the three-dimensional framework, the end of someone's temporal existence is the end of someone's existence *period*" (128). Silverstein, somehow, has managed to muddle the very approach to the question of the nonexistence of the dead that he put forward as a relativistic, four-dimensional alternative to presentism, which, unlike four-dimensionalism, is compelled to confront, head-on, the paradox of nonexistence. Having endorsed Quine's statement that "in four-dimensional space-time . . . all [people are seen] as co-existing in an *eternal and timeless sense* of the word," Silverstein turns around, amazingly, and announces that "the four-dimensional framework emphatically does *not* imply that a human being's existence itself is either *atemporal or eternal.*"

The source of the confusion appears to be Silverstein's (correct) claim that, according to four-dimensionalism, "a human being's existence has temporal boundaries." What that means is that on this approach, one occupies during the times of one's life a specific, limited section of space-time. This is the "location" of one's life. But, as previously stated, on this approach, *where* you are—i.e. where you're located—in space-time has no effect on *whether* you are. Just because the dead have a different location in space-time than do we does not mean that, unlike us, they fail to exist, since *existence, according to four-dimensionalism, is not affected by location.* Contra Silverstein, then, the consistent four-dimensionalist *does* "deny that someone's death is the end of his existence," and thereby manages to avoid the problem of nonexistence (at least, where the dead, as well as prenatal and future people, are concerned; merely possible people are another matter).

As I said earlier, however, relativity is not the end of the story on how one should approach the question of what the correct theory of time tells us about death and nonexistence, even if we accept arguments like Gödel's that relativity, conventionally understood, including by Einstein himself, implies temporal idealism, or at least four-dimensionalism. For one thing, if, as Gödel and others have argued, relativity, in particular special relativity, is inconsistent with the intuitive concept of time, understood as implying presentism, isn't this as much an argument demonstrating that something is lacking in relativity as it is an argument that something is amiss with presentism? As Plato is alleged to have said, a sound theory should be able to "save the phenomena," and the phenomena here are the passing of time and the reality of change. As the philosopher of science Tim Maudlin said in a recent interview, "Physics has discovered some really strange things about the world, but it has not discovered that change is an illusion. . . . Go to the man on the street and ask whether time has a direction, whether the future is different from the past, and whether time doesn't march on toward the future. That's the natural view. The more interesting view is how the physicists manage to convince themselves that time doesn't have a direction."[22] In "Remarks on the Passing of Time,"[23] he notes that "[n]ot infrequently, the

22. Maudlin 2017.

23. Maudlin 2001.

notion of the passage of time is discussed under the rubric, 'time's flow', or 'the moving now'. These locutions tend to be favored by authors intent on dismissing the notion. . . . Except in a metaphorical sense, time does not move or flow. Rivers flow and locomotives move. Of course, rivers only flow and locomotives only move *because time passes*" (260; emphasis added). It is often said that locomotives move insofar as they occupy different places at different times, and this is indeed so, *as long as the times themselves are passing.* Rivers flow relative to riverbanks, but there's nothing relative to which time passes.

Maudlin himself believes this is consistent with relativity, *correctly*—i.e. unconventionally—*understood.* The conventional geometrical background of relativity, he believes, must be rethought. To return to his interview: "Standard geometry just wasn't developed for the purpose of doing space-time. It was developed for the purpose of just doing spaces, and spaces have no directedness in them. And then you took this formal tool that you developed for this one purpose and then pushed it to this other purpose."[24] (See his *New Foundations for Physical Geometry: The Theory of Linear Structures* [2014].)

---

24. Compare what I wrote in *Gödel Meets Einstein* (1999): "Whereas the mathematicians, following Plato's lead, were doing their best to take time out of mathematics . . . the physicists were busy reintroducing this temporally purified mathematics into (theory of) time. Thus the physicists of time have been employing an instrument designed expressly, by the mathematicians, to be insensitive to the temporal!" I quote immediately after this what Milič Čapek wrote in *The Philosophical Impact of Contemporary Physics*: "Only when succession and change are incorporated into the very foundations of geometry is there a better chance of expressing the dynamic nature of becoming" (1961, 35).

And others, too, are rethinking relativity. Mark Hinchcliff, for example, in "A Defense of Presentism in a Relativistic Setting,"[25] discussing a suggestion of Prior's, asks us to consider a "'neo-Lorentzian' theory" that will, he believes, "accommodate the same experimental results as the special theory, and it comes with absolute simultaneity. It is thus a way to fit the special theory—or a theory with the same experimental consequences—into a presentist setting" (S585). He points out that "[a]n obvious objection to this view is that it cannot be experimentally determined which inertial frames are at absolute rest" (S585), adding that "Prior seems willing to live with this consequence" (S585), as, it seems, is Hinchcliff.

Speaking of Lorentz, one should recall what the renowned physicist J. S. Bell wrote, much earlier, in "How to Teach Special Relativity,"[26] which resonates with Hinchcliff's suggestion. "Since it is experimentally impossible," writes Bell, "to say which of two uniformly moving systems is *really* at rest, Einstein declares the notions 'really resting' and 'really moving' as meaningless. . . . Lorentz, on the other hand, preferred the view that there is indeed a state of *real* rest, defined by the 'aether,' even though the laws of physics conspire to prevent us from identifying it experimentally. *The facts of physics do not oblige us to accept one philosophy rather than the other*" (77; emphasis added). Once again, a cautionary tale about how careful one must be when attempting to draw philosophical conclusions from physical theory.

One should also remember, of course, that physics includes not just relativity but quantum mechanics, especially

25. Hinchcliff 2000.

26. Bell 1989.

since the two theories are yet to be fully reconciled with one other. And the role of time in quantum mechanics, especially with regard to the so-called collapse of the wave function and quantum-mechanical entanglement, differs from that in relativity.[27] As Popper wrote a while ago,[28] commenting on the experimental results of Alain Aspect and others concerning Bell's theorem, "[S]hould the result of these experiments . . . be accepted, and interpreted as establishing action at a distance (with infinite velocity), then these experiments would have to be regarded as the first crucial experiments between Lorentz's and Einstein's interpretations of special relativity" (54). One could object to this line of thinking, however, as Abner Shimony did:[29] "[Q]uantum-mechanical nonlocality 'peacefully coexists' with special relativity theory, because quantum-mechanical correlations between spatially separated systems cannot be exploited for sending messages faster than light" (286). But Popper anticipated this kind of response: "[E]ven if signals cannot

27. See, for example, "Quantum Gravity's Time Problem," by N. Wolchover (2016).

She writes, "Theoretical physicists striving to unify quantum mechanics and general relativity . . . face what's called 'the problem of time.' In quantum mechanics, time is universal and absolute; its steady ticks dictate the evolving entanglements between particles. But in general relativity . . . time is relative and dynamical, a dimension that's inextricably interwoven with directions x, y and z into a four-dimensional 'space-time' fabric. The fabric warps under the weight of matter, causing nearby stuff to fall toward it (this is gravity), and slowing the passage of time relative to clocks far away."

28. "A Critical Note on the Greatest Days of Quantum Theory" (Popper 1984).

29. "The Transient Now" (Shimony 1993).

be transmitted with infinite velocity, the mere idea of infinite velocity requires the existence of a Lorentzian-Newtonian absolute space and absolute time, although, as Newton anticipated, it may not be possible in this case to identify the inertial system that is absolutely at rest" (1984, 54).

In the same vein, more recently, David Albert and Rivka Galche, in "Was Einstein Wrong? A Quantum Threat to Special Relativity,"[30] draw attention to the fact that in *Quantum Non-locality and Relativity*,[31] Maudlin argues forcefully that the "peaceful coexistence" Shimony claimed is not quite so peaceful. They point, further, to a recent result of Albert's that creates more problems for coexistence. "The trouble," they write, "is that special relativity tends to mix up space and time in a way that transforms quantum-mechanical entanglement among distinct physical systems into something along the lines of an entanglement among physical situations at different times—something that in a perfectly concrete way exceeds or eludes or has nothing to do with any sum of situations at distinct temporal instants." (39) They conclude that "[t]he status of special relativity, just more than a century after it was presented to the world, is suddenly a radically open and radically developing question." (39)

The role of time, then, in contemporary physics, in relativity and in quantum mechanics and in the relationship between the two, is a "radically open question,"[32] as is, in

30. Albert and Rivka 2009.

31. Maudlin 1994.

32. Of the voluminous literature on the subject, I draw attention to Christian Wüthrich, "The Fate of Presentism in Modern Physics" (2013), and Michael Esfeld, "Quantum Physics and Presentism" (2015). (I thank Dustin Lazarovici for directing me toward these two articles.) For a recent

particular, the question of absolute simultaneity and instantaneous action at a distance, and indeed, the question of the passing of time. It would clearly be a hasty and premature conclusion to draw, then, from "what physics teaches us," that we're free to ignore what Maudlin says "the man on the street" would tell us if we were to ask whether "time doesn't march on toward the future," bringing with it a change in existence. One cannot, as is so often done, not least by Einstein himself, affirm, blithely, that time, in the sense that distinguishes past, present, and future, is an illusion, and then calmly go back to smoking one's pipe, as if one's view of the world has not been thrown into a cocked hat. I remain a temporal chauvinist, but at the same time, I believe there remains the task Gödel put before us, to see whether our intuition of time can be reconciled with time as it appears in physics, just as, within physics itself, there remains the task of reconciling relativity with quantum mechanics. (Indeed, the two tasks may well be intimately related.) Einstein's reputation will not suffer if we acknowledge that it's too soon to declare that he succeeded in uncoupling death from nonexistence.

philosophical defense of presentism, see Craig Bourne, *A Future for Presentism* (2006). For a philosophical critique, see M. Joshua Mozersky, *Time, Language, and Ontology: The World from the B-Theoretic Perspective* (2015). Note that even Mozersky doesn't want to deny that there's a sense in which time passes: "I want to suggest," he writes, that "the passage of time is the *B-theoretic ordering of events* by the (semantically basic) 'is earlier than' relation: that's it. On the B-series, first one thing happens, then another. That is temporal passage" (168; emphasis added). For a point of view that differs from both Bourne and Mozersky, see Bradford Skow, *Objective Becoming* (2015).

VIII

FELLOW TRAVELERS

> The existential quantifier [I'm using] is not restricted to individuals that exist. It includes non-existent individuals.
>
> —NATHAN SALMON

WHEN CLIMBING A MOUNTAIN, WHETHER physical or metaphysical, it's good to pause as you approach the summit to take in the view, to see how far you've come. It's time, then, to provide an overview of where I've arrived in trying to establish what I believe is a fresh perspective on the metaphysics of death. With that picture in place, I'll take note of my agreements and disagreements with fellow travelers who, in various ways and in varying degrees, are taking a similar path up the mountain.

I believe that the paradox of nonexistence, which goes back to Parmenides, is not a pseudoproblem. It represents a serious challenge that demands an answer in metaphysics, generally, and more specifically, in the metaphysics of death. My response to the question posed by Quine—what is it that there is not?—is *the nonexistent*. There are things that fail to exist—the dead, for example—although there don't *exist* things that fail to exist. Existence isn't all there is. The existents aren't all there are. We need to distinguish existence from what underlies both existence and nonexistence, which we can follow tradition and call *being*.

The paradox of nonexistence is not resolved by Russell's theory of descriptions. *Pace* Frege and Russell, there is a predicate of existence that applies to individuals, which we can represent thus: **E(x)**. It must be taken as primitive. In particular, it is not definable using the existential quantifier, which, as I use it, expresses not existence but being. To state, formally, that there are things that don't exist, I write: **(∃x)~E(x)**. Quine misstated the paradox of nonexistence. He should have stated it thus: "Nonexistents must in some sense be, otherwise, what is it that is not?" The resolution of the paradox is then that it is true that nonexistents must in some sense be, but that sense is not existence, but being.

Parmenides, correctly understood, was thus adumbrating the truth that, at the deepest level, nothing—no thing, no being—ever comes to be or passes away except into and out of *existence*. Being, unlike existence, is unerasable. If there are such things as individuals, and you are one of them, you can't be "rubbed out," not even by death, indeed, not even by failing to be born. Parmenides was not, however, a precursor of Meinong. *Pace* Meinong, what is loosely described as the nonexistence of Aphrodite, a "fictional object," is not a fact about a genuine individual, Aphrodite, who happens not to exist. There is no such person as the Greek goddess Aphrodite.[1] I agree with Kripke, against other philosophers

---

1. Whether there are Greek gods in the sense of abstract creations of mythmakers, as is maintained by Kripke, Salmon, Thomasson, et al., I leave as an open question. I certainly don't believe, however, what Salmon has said, that a fictional character is literally *part of* the story in which it (or should I say, he or she?) appears. Stories consist of words, or thoughts, or ideas, not fictional people, just as paintings consist of paint, not people, fictional or otherwise. Nor do I concur with Salmon in maintaining that the author of a story, as opposed to its readers, was, in that story, referring to a

studying fiction, that the proper analysis of such negative existentials is an as yet unresolved problem. It's a problem, however, in the philosophy of language, not metaphysics. By contrast, the nonexistence of Socrates—both before birth and after death—is a fact about a genuine individual, namely, Socrates. How it stands with Socrates determines whether or not he exists.

An individual may fail to exist because he or she is merely possible, or because he or she no longer or not yet exists. When possible persons become actual, they don't *travel* from one possible world to another. What happens in one possible world has no effect on another. The way an individual enters this world depends on the type of individual it is. Buildings are built, statues are sculpted, and human beings are (usually) created by sexual intercourse. If people fail to exist because they're not yet born or have died, their fate has been determined by their position in time—at least, if time is what we intuitively take it to be. But is time what we intuitively take it to be? In spite of what has seemed to be the clear message delivered by the theory of relativity, the question of the nature of time, in light of modern physics, turns out to be a fraught one. Given how strong are our intuitions about time's passage and direction, and the fact that physics, to date, has not succeeded in "saving the phenomena," wisdom counsels us not to abandon intuitive time unless, somehow, forced to—in which case, so to speak, *all bets are off*.[2] I am thus a

fictional character, an abstract object he or she made up. Authors pretend to refer to real people. They don't really refer to pretend people. See Mark Sainsbury, *Fiction and Fictionalism* (2010).

2. Unlike Einstein, Gödel concluded that in a sense all bets *are* off, that the ordinary "empiricist" or "realist" view of ourselves and the world needed

temporal chauvinist—what is often called a presentist. The present isn't just one time among others.

Nor is the actual world just one world among others. I am also a modal chauvinist, though not an actualist, as that term is usually understood. Only the actual world exists. But times other than the present, worlds other than the actual, though they lack existence or actuality, are nevertheless real. There are other times; there are other possible worlds. They possess not existence but being. They aren't, however, of a different *kind* than what happens to exist. *Existents do not constitute a species, distinct from nonexistents*—a fact Kant drew attention to, long ago, though his insight has not been appreciated. What distinguishes existents from nonexistents is only their *existence*, not their *nature* or *essence*. It's not *what* they are that separates the living from the dead, but *that* they are.

The dead are nonexistent objects, nonexistent people, as are the unborn and merely possible people. They are the same kind of objects as the living, i.e. persons, concrete (if

---

to be radically revised, in the spirit of "idealists" like Plato and Leibniz. Popper (1982, 3, note 2) says that he discussed "A Remark about the Relationship between Relativity Theory and Idealistic Philosophy" (Gödel 1990) with Einstein: "The reality of time and change seemed to me to be the crux of realism. [Einstein] clearly disagreed with Gödel's idealism[, and] I tried to present to Einstein-Parmenides as strongly as I could my conviction that a clear stand must be made against any idealistic view of time. . . . I argued that we should not be swayed by our theories to give up common sense too easily. Einstein clearly did not want to give up realism (for which the strongest arguments were based on common sense), though I think he was ready to admit, as I was, that we might be forced one day to give it up if very powerful arguments (of Gödel's type, say) were to be brought against it." Note that, as discussed earlier, Gödel believed that it wasn't he but Einstein who had (so to speak, inadvertently) demonstrated the ideality of time.

persons are concrete), living (i.e. organic, though not actually alive). *Concreteness* must not be confused with *actuality*.
Actuality concerns *whether* you are. Concreteness concerns
what you are. Essence is not existence. Essence, *pace* Sartre,
"precedes" existence.

What Plato said in *The Phaedo* was right: opposites come
from opposites, the living come from "the dead"—i.e. the
prenatal nonexistent—just as the dead come from the living.
Pace Peirce and Prior, the existent emerge not from *a cloud of
generality* but rather from *raindrops of individuality*. It's not
true that actuality alone—i.e. existence—collapses the pure
generality of nonexistence. The preexistent are individuals,
just like you and me. I endorse, *contra* Marcus and Thomson,
Peirce and Prior, the Principle of Prior Possibility: *nothing
becomes actual unless previously possible*. Your parents are responsible for your actuality, not your possibility.

To make sense of possibility and actuality, one needs
to invoke possible worlds, and by "possible worlds" I mean
possible (concrete) *worlds*, not actual (abstract) *states* or
histories of "the world." A world is a maximal possible situation or state of affairs. As Barwise and Perry insist, a situation
is something that is in a sense concrete, not something abstract like a property. Merely possible worlds are individuals,
just like the actual world. Lewis is right that they are in some
sense concrete, no less than the actual world, but Stalnaker
is also right, contra Lewis, that other possible worlds aren't
actual (though Lewis is right that they're actual *relative* to
themselves). I reject Lewis's principle of the indexicality of
actuality—that actuality, as such, is relative. Actuality as
such (*pace* Lewis), existence as such (*pace* Parsons), is absolute. Contra Lewis, possible worlds aren't *concrete existents*,
and contra Stalnaker, they aren't *abstract existents*. Rather,

possible worlds are **concrete nonexistents**. And the same is true of possible persons (if persons are concrete objects). If Stalnaker is a self-described "moderate realist," I must be an "immoderate realist," though not in Lewis's sense.

Possible worlds, however, do not, so to speak, contain the whole story. Not all facts that obtain are "contained" in the actual world. Stalnaker was wrong to say that "the actual world" is just another name for reality. Following Fine, I believe we should distinguish worldly facts, which determine how things stand with regard to a particular world, from transcendental facts, which constitute the "framework" or "background" of possible worlds. Transcendental facts concern how things are independently of what occurs within any given world. They determine, as it were, the nature of things, not how individuals happen to fare in a given world. That Kripke is a person is a transcendental fact. That Kripke is actually a logician and a philosopher concerns how it stands with Kripke in this, the actual world. In a Kripke-less world, the fact that he doesn't exist in that world is contained in that world. Kripke himself is a constituent of that fact even though he doesn't exist in that world, because for an individual to be a constituent of a fact or a world—or a set—what is necessary is not that there *exist* such a person, but only that there *be* such an individual.[3]

There is another fact, however, that seems to be neither worldly nor transcendental, namely, the fact that this world, our world, in which Kripke exists, itself exists or is actual.

3. For a thoughtful account of what it is to be a constituent of a fact, see Keith Hossack, *The Metaphysics of Knowledge* (2007): "The relation of *combination* that obtains between a fact and its constituents is *sui generis*; the terminology of 'combination' and 'constituents' should not be taken to have mereological connotations" (45). See also Plantinga, "Existentialism" (2007).

Given *the contingency of actuality*, this isn't a transcendental fact, a fixture within the framework of possible worlds. But neither is it a worldly fact, a fact contained within the actual world itself or within some other possible world. Whether or not a possible world is actual is not determined by *how things stand according to that world*, itself, any more than whether or not a proposition is true is determined by what is the case according to that proposition, itself (as Frege pointed out). Where, then, is that fact to be found? This is, as far as I know, an unsolved problem.

There remain, then, unresolved problems with regard to the concept of possible worlds, but these problems do not suffice, I believe, to justify abandoning that important concept. What important concept, after all, does not pose as yet unresolved problems? In spite of these concerns, I hope to have presented a coherent possibilist framework within which to approach the question of possible persons and the metaphysics of death, a framework that stands in stark contrast to that offered by others working in this field. There are, however, a number of points of contact with philosophers laboring in other philosophical vineyards, in particular, the foundations of QML, and more generally, philosophical logic, who, in turn, have not contributed, explicitly, to the philosophy of death. Indeed, it's been one of the principal goals of this study to draw attention to the striking lack of interaction among these fields of study. Ironically, then, it is, for the most part, philosophers working outside the field of the philosophy of death whom I consider fellow travelers in the philosophy of death. It will help, then, to further clarify my approach to situate my thoughts among the views of some key fellow travelers: Connolly, Williamson, Salmon, Fine, Kaplan, and Parfit.

Before beginning my discussion, however, I need to say a word about why I've omitted Nagel, in particular, from my list. In my first contribution to the field,[4] I expressed agreement on a number points with Nagel's seminal article "Death" (1993). I took exception, however, to his lack of commitment to the view that the dead are nonexistent objects, and his consequent failure to address—not to say, to attempt to resolve—Parmenides's paradox of nonexistence. The question Nagel and most subsequent writers have addressed, the so-called "no subject problem," is concerned not with the metaphysical question of nonexistent objects, as such—i.e. the ontology of nonexistence—but rather with the psychological/ethical question of how or whether death can be *harmful* if there is no "subject" there to *experience* deprivation. To be sure, Nagel notes that the dead used to exist, but he doesn't commit himself to the fact that since they exist no longer, they are nonexistent *tout court*, hence, are *nonexistent objects*.[5]

He shares, in this respect, the view that's become standard in the field, that one can obtain an adequate metaphysics of death "on the cheap," ontologically speaking—that

---

4. "The Dead" (1993).

5. "[I]f there is a loss [when someone dies]," writes Nagel, "someone must suffer it, and *he* must have existence and specific spatial and temporal location" ("Death," in Fischer [1993], 67). Nagel, surely, is misusing the expression "have existence." Most people, for example, would agree that you can't move into a house unless it has existence, but would not agree that a house *has* existence simply because it *used to exist* (at a "specific spatial and temporal location"). The correct way to formulate Nagel's point would be, "and *he* must *have existed* and *have had* a specific spatial and temporal location." Nagel's misformulation of his point muddies the water, clouding over the fact that the persons who suffer from death, namely, the dead, are nonexistent objects, an inconvenient fact that cries our for explanation.

one can do justice to the ontology of death without making any "extravagant metaphysical commitments." (I borrow this last phrase from Stalnaker, who employed it in a different, but related, context.) The metaphysics of death, however, comes with a high ontological price tag. There are no philosophical bargains to be had here. You have to pay market price. One cannot account for death, hence, for nonexistence, possibility, actuality, and temporality, without extending one's ontological horizons.

Let me begin, then, by comparing my views with Niall Connolly's in "How the Dead Live."⁶ I know his views accord to some extent with my own because he says so: "Palle Yourgrau has argued in two papers . . . that although the dead don't exist, they remain among us. They remain available . . . to be . . . loved. . . . The dead count as examples of *non-existent objects*. The first thing I want to do in this paper is to say why I agree with this." He concurs, as well, with my espousal of presentism, which he defends. He departs from my views, however, in describing his approach to nonexistent objects as Meinongian. Indeed, there is an extended discussion in his essay about neo-Meinongians. And a Meinongian he appears to be, even though he writes that "'Pegasus is a winged horse' may appear to be about a fact involving a winged horse. But it isn't really." He adds a footnote, however, in which he says: "Note I am denying it is about a winged horse; not that it is about Pegasus (I think Pegasus, like Socrates, is a bare particular)" (note 28). He thereby commits what I have taken to be a cardinal fallacy, *comparing Socrates with Aphrodite*, the dead with the fictional.

6. Connolly 2011.

He rejects, however, the Meinongian principle that F(*the F*). He denies that Pegasus the winged horse is a winged horse. As for the dead, Connolly believes they have no qualities at all, and "If the dead have no qualities this makes them 'bare particulars.'" This, clearly, has nothing to do with my own approach to the dead, but I can see why someone might find it appealing. Once you die, you're gone. You've disappeared. You seem to have become nothing. But at the same time you're still somehow there, to be a constituent of facts (including the fact that you don't exist), to be an object of love. How much more stripped down of being something in particular can something be while remaining a particular, one might think, than being a *bare* particular?

Tempting as this view may be, however, one should resist it. As I've been insisting, death, loss of existence, affects that you are, not what you are. Moreover, how can what remains after death be *you* if it lacks not only your accidental properties but even your essential ones? After all, Aristotle came up with the distinction between accidental and essential properties precisely to explain continuity through change.

Connolly, unsurprisingly, is aware of this objection. "My position," he says, "is radically anti-essentialist. A thing of a kind does not belong to that kind in every possible situation in which it is to be found. . . . However, my views are compatible with the view that a thing of a kind belongs to that kind in every possible situation in which it *exists*. . . . The change involved in ceasing to exist has to be a radical change. . . . [I]n ceasing to exist one becomes a mere non-entity" (note 49). He goes on to say that "[i]f death doesn't involve the elimination of its subject, what is so bad about death? If Socrates is, for example, still a person, or still a philosopher, why is Socrates so unfortunate?"

In response, I would say first that I can't make sense of something losing its essence and yet remaining the self-same thing. Second, being a philosopher, though it was obviously a very *important* trait during his life, is not an *essential* trait of Socrates. If during his life he had become a painter, divorced his wife, and separated himself from Plato, he would still have existed—he would still have been Socrates. By contrast, assuming being a person is an essential* trait of Socrates, he could never lose it. To be a person is to be the kind of being that, when it exists, is capable of thought, of communication, of loving, of being moral, etc. Of course, since, upon dying, Socrates ceased to exist, he ceased being capable (i.e. *actually* capable) of thought, of communication, of love, etc., which is why he's now so "unfortunate." Recall the distinction between being a *living-being* (i.e. an organic object) and being (actually) *alive*—i.e. actually exercising the functions of nutrition, digestion, reproduction, etc.

The issue here concerns what it *means* to belong to a kind. Something belongs to the kind living-thing just in case it can't exist without being alive. That's the *kind*—living-thing. Socrates belongs to it, even after death. Even after death, that is, it's true of Socrates that *he can't exist unless he's alive.* Connolly, however, says: no, after death, Socrates *no longer belongs to that kind (or any other).* But to belong to that kind just means that one can't exist without being alive, and *that's still true of Socrates.* It's not only true of Socrates *when he exists.* Yet Connolly says that "a thing of a kind belongs to that kind in every possible situation in which it *exists*"—i.e. *only* when it exists.

Belonging to a kind is part of something's essence* or nature, which it can't lose, not even by ceasing to exist. We speak of dead philosophers and also of dead people.

The surface linguistic similarity obscures the metaphysical truth. A dead philosopher, like Socrates, is someone who philosophized *when* he actually existed. A dead person is someone who exhibits the traits of personhood *whenever* they exist. A dead person is not something with no qualities, a mere bare particular.

In spite of Connolly's agreement with me, then, that the dead are nonexistent objects, there is much that separates my approach from his. By contrast, in spite of Timothy Williamson's disagreement with me in "Nonexistents"[7] about whether the dead are nonexistent objects, there's much that unites my approach with his. His argument (233–34) runs thus:

(1) Necessarily, if I do not exist then the proposition that I do not exist exists.

(2) Necessarily, if the proposition that I do not exist is true then the proposition that I do not exist exists.

(3) Necessarily, if the proposition that I do not exist exists then I exist.

(4) Necessarily, if I do not exist then I exist.

Conclusion: "Necessarily, I exist." This argument, if valid, would obviously apply to everything. By Williamson's lights, then, everything *necessarily* exists; a much stronger claim than Quine's, that everything *exists*.

Williamson defends (3) by saying that "if I did not exist, there would be nothing for the proposition to state the non-existence of" (234). That's a version of Parmenides's paradox

7. Williamson 2002.

of nonexistence as formulated by Quine. Williamson resolves the paradox by rejecting *nonexistence* in favor of *necessary existence*. By contrast, I resolve the paradox by *retaining nonexistence*, but distinguishing *existence* from *being*. Williamson is an unreconstructed Parmenidean. I am a modified Parmenidean. Clearly, there is a deep similarity between our views, but at the same time, also a deep dissimilarity—there being a deep dissimilarity, after all, between necessary existence and nonexistence!

The similarity, and at the same time, the difference between Williamson's views and my own is evident throughout his essay. He states, for example, that "if a given item had not existed, then there would have been no such item" (244), and that "if x does not exist, then there is no such item as x" (244). By contrast, I hold that even if Socrates had not existed, there would have been such a person as Socrates, because, unlike Williamson, I think the quantifier *there is an F*, in natural language—formalized as, $(\exists x)(Fx)$—expresses not *existence* but *being*, and that existence is expressed by a primitive predicate, (Ex). Thus, whereas Williamson says, "We can therefore symbolize 'x exists' by the familiar formula $\exists y\, x = y$" (244), I symbolize "x exists" by the formula "$E(x)$" (and thus "x doesn't exist" by "$\sim E(x)$").

And yet, having distinguished Williamson's views from my own, I note that he goes on to say that he's speaking here of "the *logical* sense of 'exist'" (244; emphasis added), which sounds a lot like what I'm calling *being*. Indeed, it is a lot like what I'm calling being. But there remains a crucial difference. As I've been emphasizing throughout this study, *being* is not a form of *existence*, whether Williamson's "logical sense of existence" or Kaplan's "attenuated being" of nonexistents (to be contrasted with the "robust being" enjoyed by you and me). I want, with Quine, to retain the good old term "exist," and to draw a sharp line between being and existence, and thus not to sweep the paradox of nonexistence under the rug. In a sense, Williamson, too, wants to avoid sweeping. "Doubtless," he says, "*in some sense* Trajan no longer exists" (245). I agree. But I say the sense in which Trajan no longer exists is . . . nonexistence!

What further separates Williamson's views from my own is how he characterizes the sense in which Trajan fails to exist. Trajan, he says, qua nonexistent, "lacks spatial location," "is no longer concrete," has become something "neither abstract nor concrete." Trajan, he says, is "an ex-concrete object." As I've been insisting, however, one should not conflate concreteness with existence. Concreteness concerns *what* you are, existence concerns *whether* you are. As I emphasized above in my discussion of Connolly, when you die, you sacrifice your existence, not your essence. Trajan, even in death, remains a concrete object, which means that he can't exist without occupying space, being solid, engaging in causal relations with other objects, having a carbon footprint, etc. *Pace* Connolly and, it seems, Williamson, that's true of him now, not only when he exists. That's simply the kind of being Trajan is, and nothing, including death and nonexistence, can cause you to cease being the kind of being you are. (And I remind you: *existents do not constitute a kind of being, a species.*)

Williamson rejects talk of what kind of thing Trajan *is*, now that he's dead and nonexistent and a merely possible physical object. "Someone might still ask," he says, "'What *kind* of thing is a merely possible physical object?' The answer that 'possible physical object' already demarcates a kind is liable to elicit the complaint 'I asked what it *is*, not what it *could have been'"* (247). Williamson's reply to such a complaint is that "[w]hen we think of past physical objects, we are content to classify them in terms of what they *were*; we do not insist on a classification it terms of what they are *now*, without reference to the past. Why should possible physical objects be different?" (247; emphasis added). This is close to my own view, but, as indicated by my discussion of Connolly, not identical. There remains the subtle difference I want to insist on between Trajan's no longer belonging to the kind, *physical object*, though he now belongs to the kind, *possible physical object* (Williamson's view) and Trajan's still belonging to the kind, physical object (my own view), in virtue of the fact that whenever he exists, he exhibits the traits of physicality. But if the distinction between the two views is so subtle, why do I insist on it? I insist on it because I hold firm to my belief that death, hence nonexistence, changes that you are, not what you are.

And yet there remains, once again, a concordance between Williamson's views and my own if I modify his affirmation that "if my parents had never met, I would have been something neither abstract nor concrete, but something that could have been concrete. I would not have been a physical object but I would have been a possible physical object" (246). Though I disagree with him about exactly *what* I would have been had my parents never met, what's crucial here is our agreement that even if my parents hadn't met, there *would have been* such a person as myself who could have existed. This is an instance of my principle that nothing becomes actual unless previously possible, which as we've seen, appears to be rejected by Prior, Peirce and Marcus, and a host of others. It follows, I might add, that on the view advocated by Williamson and myself (and also, at least at one time, by

Derek Parfit), if my parents hadn't met, I would have been prevented from existing .[8] By contrast, the vast majority of philosophers who have confronted this issue have insisted that had my parents never met, there would have been no *me* to be denied existence.

Which brings me to my next fellow traveler, the afore-mentioned Parfit. In his appendix "On What There Is" (2011), he says that "[r]ather than being *Actualists* who believe: There is nothing except what actually exists, we ought to be *Possibilitists*, who believe: *There are* some things that are merely possible" (719).[9] That sounds very much like my own view. What, however, does Parfit mean by "there are"? He's at pains to defend the thesis that nothing prevents us from considering both a narrow sense of "exists," according to which only what is actual exists, and a wide sense, including what merely possibly exists. He suggests that when one says that there are some things that are merely possible, "there are" should be read as expressing the wide sense of existence. He opposes what he calls "the Actualist Single Sense View" that " 'there are' must mean 'there actually exist' " (723). On the contrary, he says that "we claim that, though there is one wide sense in which there are both actual objects and objects that are merely possible, it is only the actual objects that also exist in the narrower, actualist sense" (728).

As I said, this sounds very much like my own view that we should acknowledge possible objects by insisting that *there are* such objects, though there *exist* only actual objects.

---

8. I'm assuming for the sake of argument that I could only have come into existence through the agency of my parents.

9. As will be seen in the following chapter, however, in a late essay, Parfit appears to have reversed his position with regard to possible people.

If one looks closely at what Parfit is saying, however, it becomes clear that, though, so to speak, the spirit of Parfit's proposal resembles my own, strictly speaking there is an important difference. Parfit appears to be suggesting when one says there are merely possible objects, one is invoking *existence*, only in a wider sense than when one says that only actual objects exist. In other words, Parfit does not, as I've been attempting to do, distinguish what *exists* from what is *nonexistent* but still has *being*, but rather introduces *two modes of existence*. Whereas, on my account, possibility and actuality represent two different *modes of being*, for Parfit, they represent two different *forms of existence*. The paradox of nonexistence, once again, has been sidestepped.

And there's a further problem. The basis of Parfit's reasoning, that we're free to extend the sense of "exists," is a weak move. It's a free country, as they say, so Parfit is right that no one can prevent us from extending the sense of "exists"—or, in indeed, of any other term—as we please. The question is, what exactly is accomplished by doing so? My answer: little or nothing. We're free to extend the term "fish" so that it applies to whales, but not only would we accomplish nothing by doing so, we would sacrifice the value of having a classificatory scheme that reflects important biological facts—such as that unlike those creatures that are now classified as fish, whales are mammals—in favor of an alternative classification scheme that reflects the more superficial fact that, like fish, whales live in the sea.

I'm unhappy, thus, with Parfit's reasoning in terms of extending the sense of "exists," but, at the same time, as I've indicated, I think the spirit of his proposal is very close to that of my own. It remains, however, that, in company with Williamson and Kaplan, Parfit fails to acknowledge the concept of *being*—a bridge between existence and nonexistence—and thus, like them, fails to address the paradox of nonexistence.

Finally, although Parfit provides a number of compelling examples of merely possible objects we need to take into account in making plans for the future, he isn't always as careful as he should be in claiming to refer to a specific merely possible object. I'm thinking of his example (D): "There was a palace designed by Wren to replace the burnt Palace of Whitehall" (721). According to Parfit, of this claim "we can truly say (E): There was such a possible palace designed by Wren, but this palace was not built and never actually existed" (721). The question is, was there really a specific possible object, *the* palace designed by Wren, which was never built and thus never became actual?

I had to look this up. I read on a blog, *Exploring London*,[10] that "[f]ollowing the restoration, in the 1660's King Charles II apparently had Sir Christopher Wren quietly draw up plans to redevelop the palace, but these weren't followed through, although during the reign of King James II he did work on several projects at the palace. . . . In 1698, much of the bloated Whitehall Palace . . . burnt down. . . . The then king, King William III, approached Wren and he again submitted plans for its rebuilding. . . . But Wren's plans . . . were largely never realized . . . and the destroyed palace never rebuilt." It's far from clear, from this account, that there is a specific possible object that can be correctly described as *the* palace designed by Wren which was never built. Wren certainly, at different times, worked on plans for *a* rebuilt palace, but it's not clear

---

10. https://exploring-london.com/2014/11/26/8-structures-from-the-london-that-never-was-4-whitehall-palace-remodelled/.

here is such a thing as *the* palace designed by Wren that was never built.

If the spirit behind Parfit's appendix is concordant with my own, not just the spirit but the letter of Nathan Salmon's essays "Existence," "Nonexistence," and "What Is Existence?" (2008a, 2008b, 2014) accord well with my approach. In "Nonexistence," for example, Salmon writes that "[i]n . . . negative existentials [like 'Socrates does not exist'] there is some sense in which the subject term refers to a definite nonexistent thing: a past, future, merely possible, or impossible object. . . . The negative existentials say of these definite things, correctly, that they do not exist" (85). Further, like me, he rejects Meinong: "I am not making the Meinongian claim that any description, even if logically contradictory, refers to some possible or impossible object" (48).

He denies, also, the principle advanced by many that existence is a precondition for having properties: "This principle that existence is a pre-condition for having properties—that existence precedes suchness—is a confused and misguided prejudice. . . . Socrates does not exist in my present circumstance, yet he has numerous properties here—for example, being mentioned and discussed by me" (66). In rejecting the principle that "existence precedes suchness" and affirming, in "Existence" (49), that "predication precedes existence," he's in agreement with me that essence precedes existence. (If predication in general precedes existence, so must essential predication.)

And as previously noted, against Frege and Russell, Salmon accepts the idea of a predicate of existence that applies (and sometimes fails to apply) to individual objects. He does not, however, as far as I tell, distinguish being from existence, nor does he, to my knowledge, provide an explicit account of the ontological status of nonexistents, though he's happy to quantify over them: "The existential quantifier [I'm using] is not restricted to individuals that exist. It includes non-existent individuals" ("What Is Existence?," 246). If, for Salmon, the range of the existential quantifier is not restricted to existents, what exactly does that quantifier represent? When I assert $(\exists x){\sim}E(x)$, I explain that ${\sim}E(x)$ means that x lacks the property of existence, and that $(\exists x)$, the existential quantifier, expresses *being*. What does Salmon say? As remarked earlier, in a footnote he suggests that perhaps, when it comes to impossible objects, one should employ substitutional, as opposed to objectual, quantification, an odd choice, as I also noted, for how to represent impossible *objects*. And is this suggestion meant to apply only to impossible objects, or also to merely possible objects?

Further, together with Ishiguro, Salmon wrongly criticizes Kant's important doctrine that the actual contains no more than the possible, and as a consequence, fails to distinguish concreteness from actuality. And we part company, too, on the question of set or class existence. As noted earlier, he asks us to "Consider any class that has me as an element, {Nathan Salmon}, for example (the unit class that has me as its only element). When I am dead and gone, this class will no longer exist." I, by contrast, as indicated previously, hold that the existence of a class is determined by whether "there are" such objects as its elements. Since there always was such a being as Nathan Salmon, and always will be, the existence of {Nathan Salmon}, unlike Nathan Salmon, himself, is secure. It will not pass away when Nathan Salmon does.

Kit Fine's views, in turn, like Salmon's, resemble mine in crucial, though not all, respects. We agree that, on the surface, at least, there's a problem with the Stalnaker-Kripke view of possible worlds insofar as it seems to imply that the actual world = the state of the actual world, and we agree that a possible world is possibly a world, though a state of the world is not possibly a world. Even if one agrees with Hughes's argument that such objections turn on an ambiguity in what Stalnaker and Kripke mean by "possible world," there remain, I think, problems with their approach.

I'm also sympathetic, clearly, with Fine's distinction between what he calls worldly vs. transcendental facts and properties. In particular, I agree (except for his first sentence) when he says in "Necessity and Non-existence" (2005), "I do not believe that the essence of an object is wholly given by its transcendental features. But I do believe the transcendental essence of an object constitutes a kind of skeletal 'core' from which the rest of the essence can be derived. . . . [T]he identity of an object is independent of how things turn out, not just in the relatively trivial sense that the self-identity of the object is independent of how things turn out . . . Rather, it is the core essential features of the object that will be independent of how things turn out and they will be independent in the sense of holding *regardless* of the circumstances, not *whatever* the circumstances. The objects enter the world with their identity predetermined, as it were; and there is nothing in *how* things are that can have any bearing on *what* they are" (348–49; last two emphases added).

Like me, Fine questions the relationship between the existential quantifier and existence, and talks explicitly about being versus existence. At the same time, his views are complex, and his use of terminology is sometimes at variance with my own, so that it would take a small book (or perhaps a big one) to sort out, once a common language has been found, exactly where our viewpoints on existence, being, worlds, and essence agree and disagree. Nevertheless, it's clear enough that, so to speak, he's fishing in the same metaphysical waters as I am.

Which brings me to my final fellow traveler. Unlike Fine, David Kaplan doesn't explicitly recognize the distinction between being and existence, but he comes very close when he says, as discussed earlier: "I have in mind future individuals and merely possible individuals. Such putative entities are *nonexistent. . . . Past individuals* are also, in my view, nonexistent. . . . It would then be natural to add *a narrow existence predicate* to distinguish the robust being of true local existents, like you and me, from *the more attenuated being* of the nonexistents" (607, note 101, and 608; first emphasis in the original). Past individuals are, presumably, dead, so Kaplan is here agreeing with me that the dead are individuals that don't exist, i.e. nonexistent objects, though he doesn't draw attention to the relevance of his views to the metaphysics of death. This may explain, at least in part, why philosophers working on the metaphysics of death have failed to address his ideas, ideas that in the foundations of QML have been widely discussed.

Finally, though he comes close to acknowledging explicitly the distinction between being and existence, he doesn't go very far into the ontology of being. In particular, there's no exploration of the idea that being is a bridge between existence and nonexistence, and no attempt—at least that I can discover—to resolve Parmenides's paradox of nonexistence.

So much, then, for the concordance, as well as the dissonance, between my approach to the metaphysics of death and nonexistence and the views of some key philosophers whose approach to these issues, at various points, touches my own. Clearly, in the matter of metaphysics, I'm not traveling alone. By contrast, when it comes to the philosophy of death, I have few companions. The metaphysics of death, however, is of course only part of the story. There remain questions of ethics, and more generally, questions regarding the human significance of death, to which I'll turn my attention in the next, and final, chapter.

IX

BEYOND METAPHYSICS

And how dieth the wise man? As the fool.

—ECCLESIASTES

AS I SAID AT THE BEGINNING, this is a book about the metaphysics of death. I've steered clear, not entirely, but for the most part, of ethical and religious questions. Ethics, however, isn't free of metaphysical commitments. A faulty metaphysics can inspire a faulty ethics, or less ominously, it may lead one to misrepresent the grounds on which one's ethical commitments rest.[1] A good example of this is the question of how to decide what to do when one's actions will affect who will exist and who won't. A great deal has been written about this in ethical discussions, but much of the reasoning, here, I believe, has rested on a shaky metaphysical foundation. One may reasonably believe that not bringing a nonexistent person to life doesn't harm that person, or if there be harm, that it's permissible harm. But one is not free to ground this belief on the assumption that there is no one "there" to be

---

1. Compare Frege in *The Foundations of Arithmetic* (Frege 1980): often, the question isn't the *truth* of arithmetic statements, but the *grounds* upon which they rest. Frege wasn't trying to convince us of the truth that 2 + 2 = 4, but rather to show us the grounds upon which this proposition logically rests. Similarly, if it's true that deciding not to have a child doesn't wrong the child one would have had, the question is: why is this true?

harmed, that there are no nonexistent persons who may or may not make it to existence, depending on our decisions.

As far as I can tell, however, the vast majority of philosophers who have considered this question have made this assumption, without questioning it. As I've argued, however, nothing becomes actual unless previously possible. Do those philosophers wish to deny that principle? Do they believe you can go straight to actuality, skipping possibility entirely? Do they believe your parents are responsible for both your actuality and your possibility? I hope not. Since you, my reader, are actual, you were previously possible. If you had not been created, *you*—not *something purely "general,"* as Peirce and Prior would have it, not *something of a different kind* from you—would have lacked existence, would have remained nonexistent. That may have been bad for you, or good for you, or neither, but in any case, not *because there would have been no you* to be the subject of harm or benefit.[2]

Derek Parfit, however, in his late essay "Future People, the Nonidentity Problem, and Person-Affecting Principles,"[3] does ground his assertion that never having existed, as well

---

2. Recall that my position is not simply that, given the Principle of Prior Possibility, Kripke possibly existed before he actually existed. I go further. I hold that if it's *possible* there *exists* a person = Kripke, then *there is* a person = Kripke. In symbols: $\lozenge(\exists x)(Ex \ \& \ x = \textbf{Kripke}) \supset (\exists x)(x = \textbf{Kripke})$. This should not be confused with the so-called Barcan formula (named after Ruth Barcan Marcus), which, in one form, states that $\lozenge(\exists x)(Fx) \supset (\exists x)(Fx)$. In the Barcan formula, the existential quantifier is taken to represent *existence*, whereas I take it to represent *being*. (Under the latter reading, I would affirm the Barcan formula.) Note, also, that in the antecedent in my formula, there is a proper name, "Kripke," which I take, following Kripke, to be a rigid designator, a term which refers to the same object with respect to all possible worlds.

3. Parfit 2017.

as ceasing to exist, are not a way of being badly off, on the proposition that *there are* no nonexistent people to be badly off.[4] "Like having ceased to exist, never existing is not a way of being badly off. Unlike our being killed, our never existing could not even be bad for us, or good for us, since there would have been no *us* for whom our non-existence could have been good or bad. . . . If we exist, there *is* an us. . . . We can be benefitted by being caused to exist and to have an intrinsically good life, though our non-existence would not have been worse for us" (134; first emphasis added).

Van Inwagen, in "Being, Existence, and the Ontological Argument,"[5] advances a similar view: "There are no unconceived people. And therefore there is no one whom contraception has deprived of existence" (59). And so does Kamm: "[T]here is no one who will miss out on anything if [I am] not created. . . . There will not be a subject in matters of life and death unless nonexistence comes as a change from something rather than as constant nothingness" (1993, 42 & 48). If I'm not created, however, my nonexistence would not be mere "constant nothingness." It

---

4. Nagel's views on this issue are hard to make out. "The fact that Beethoven had no children," he writes, "may have been a cause of regret to him, or a sad thing for the world, but it cannot be described as a misfortune for the children he never had. . . . [U]nless good and ill can be assigned to an embryo, or even to an unconnected pair of gametes, it cannot be said that not to be born is a misfortune" (Nagel 1993, 67). What about the question of whether it was a misfortune, not for *embryos*, but rather for the *possible people* who would have become actual had Beethoven had children? Curiously, Nagel never contemplates that question, even though, as we saw earlier, he does appear to acknowledge the fact that in some sense there are possible persons, writing that "almost every possible person has not been born and never will be" (Nagel, 1986, 211).

5. Van Inwagen 2014.

would be a state of *something*, albeit something nonexistent, namely, *me*. Since I'm in fact an actual being, I must have been, previously, a possible being. Recall what Williamson said in "Nonexistents" (2002): "[I]f my parents had never met, I would have been . . . *something* that could have been concrete. I would have been a possible concrete object" (246; emphasis added).[6] Where Williamson and I see, before Socrates's conception, a possible person who might not have been conceived even though in the course of history he was conceived , Kamm sees only constant nothingness.

Strangely, another philosopher who believes that in some sense there are possible persons who may or may not come to exist, of whom we should take account in making life-or-death decisions, is Parfit, himself, in appendix J, "On What There Is" in his earlier book (2011). Parfit, contra Parfit, as we saw in the previous chapter, opposes on both metaphysical and ethical grounds the view expressed in his later essay: "When we are making certain choices that will have effects in the further future . . . we should consider the possible effects of our different choices, not only on *actual* future people, but also on the many *possible* people who, if we had acted differently, would have later existed" (744; emphasis added). In such a case, he says, we may need to recognize that sometimes "we have acted wrongly" because "if we had acted differently, our acts would have affected some people who *never actually exist*" (744; emphasis added). We need to recognize that there are in some sense such merely possible

---

6. As I pointed out earlier, however, I depart from Williamson in holding that if your parents hadn't met, you would have been nonexistent and concrete, not merely nonexistent and *possibly* concrete. Concreteness, I repeat, should not be confused with actuality.

people, he argues, because "[i]f there was *no* sense in which there are such people, we couldn't think about them, since such thoughts would be about nothing" (745).[7]

Similar reasoning applies to abortion. One can assume an *ethical* principle like Scanlon's[8] that "the beings whom it is possible to wrong are all those who do, have, or will actually exist,"[9] and thus consistently hold that if an abortion is performed, then—if we assume that at that stage the fetus was not a person in the moral sense—one hasn't wronged the person who would have been born. But one *cannot* hold that to be true on the basis of the *metaphysical* thesis that *there is*

7. It's easy to miss the point Parfit is making here. One might be tempted to respond to what he's saying by claiming that when I reason about what to do, all I do is compare the lives of those who will *actually* exist if I do *a* with the lives of those who will *actually* exist if I do *b*. The problem, however, is that instead of using "will exist" (which implies actuality), one should be using "would exist" (which implies possibility). (1) "The people who will exist when I actually act" refers to people who will be actual in the future. But only one of the descriptions, (2) "the people who would exist if I do *a*" and (3) "the people who would exist if I do *b*" is coreferential with (1). One of them refers to merely possible people, who, if one accepts Scanlon's ethical principle (see below), can't be wronged. (In corresponding with Scanlon about this issue, I realized that this point needed to be brought out clearly.)

8. Scanlon 2000, 186–87, note 2.

9. Recall that for Quine, who spatializes time, past, present, and future people are *literally* actual people (and the only people who are actual), and given his skepticism of modality, in particular quantificational modality, there are no possible people. It's difficult, therefore, to understand how Quine can deliberate on a course of action, since for him there's no such thing as the person who would have existed if I had done a certain action. Indeed, that's exactly Parfit's point in "On What There Is" (the very title, of course, of Quine's famous essay on ontology). For Quine, it would seem, condoms are unnecessary, there being no possible people to prevent from being born.

no possible person who will thereby have been denied existence, which, as we have seen, is what Parfit does in his essay
(2017).[10]

Eli Hirsch, however, has made an interesting suggestion
in correspondence. Perhaps there's a metaphysical principle
that would be compatible with my framework, that, if true,
could be used to justify Scanlon's ethical principle. As Hirsch

---

10. There's a further issue concerning abortion, which separates it from
contraception. Even though in both cases a merely possible person failed
to make it to existence, in the case of abortion, the possible person "almost" made it to existence. So to speak, from a modal point of view, that
person's "bags were packed." Only at the last minute was the journey to
existence canceled. This seemingly hair-splitting "academic" point helps
explain, I think, why there is not infrequently an emotional trauma experienced by the would-be parents which is anything but "academic." (Of
course, needless to say, the possible person who was aborted will not have
experienced any trauma.)

Indeed, one can distinguish the degree of "investment" (or to borrow
from Quine, "modal involvement") prospective parents may have in a future child. (1) They may plan to have a child, then simply change their
minds. (2) They may plan to have a child, name it, prepare a nursery, buy
books on childrearing, etc., and only at the last minute change their minds.
(3) The situation may be as in (2), except that there is no change of mind.
The woman may become pregnant, but the pregnancy may be terminated,
for one reason or another, before (let's assume) the fetus is considered to
be, morally speaking, a person. (4) The situation may be as in (3), except
that only late in the pregnancy, when the fetus is now considered to be,
morally speaking, a person, the pregnancy is aborted (say, in order to save
the woman's life). Each stage, (1)–(4), represents a different degree of "investment" in the (or a) possible future child, with no stage representing
no investment at all. Even in stage (1), the couple may well, for the rest of
their lives, mourn the loss of what would have been their child had they
not changed their minds, and if so, they won't be guilty of committing
some sort of metaphysical blunder, there being no such thing (according
to many philosophers) as the (or a) merely possible child they might have
had. After all, if the couple had had a child, it would, obviously, have been
an actual child, and therefore it would have already been, before they had
it, a possible child.

puts it: "If x is a non-existent person, then x has numerous modal properties of the form 'could possibly be (have been) F', and x has the categorical (non-modal) property of being a person. Could x have the categorical property of 'being badly off'? One might say no on the metaphysical grounds that a non-existent thing can have only the categorical property that defines its essential nature (e.g. being a person), together, I suppose, with the categorical property of not-existing, but no other categorical property such a 'being badly off.'"

I'm inclined to respond to this suggestion as follows. The property of not-existing had certainly better be a categorical one that applies to possible people, else they wouldn't be nonexistent. Perhaps, then, to be nonexistent is, ipso facto, to be badly off.[11] Nonexistence is, all else being equal, a bad way to be. After all, Nagel, in his seminal essay, affirms that existence, as such, all else being equal, is a good way to be, and the nonexistent are deprived of that good way of being. The usual response, that this isn't the case since, when it comes to nonexistence, there's no one "there" to be badly off, doesn't hold water, since the assumption here is that there are, in some sense, nonexistent people "there" who would be badly off.

Metaphysics, thus, matters when questions of value are at issue. It matters when Kagan puts forward a possible argument against the idea that contraception prevents possible people from coming to exist based on the premise that the number of possible people who would be affected is staggeringly large. He attempts to actually work out that number, based on calculations about sperm and eggs. He concludes that "if you're going to feel sorry for [one possible

---

11. This response occurred also to Hirsch.

person], you've got to feel sorry for every merely possible person. Every person who *could* have been born but never *gets* born. And there are 3 million billion billion billion such merely possible people" (2012, 220). But that would mean, according Kagan, acknowledging that "the plight of the un-born possible people is a moral tragedy that simply staggers the mind" (221), whereas "all I can say is that it doesn't strike me as being a moral tragedy" (221).

That it doesn't strike Kagan as a moral tragedy is unsur-prising, and at the same time, unconvincing. After all, *failing to bring into existence* is not the same thing as *killing*, and our moral emotions and imaginations are simply not primed to respond to the phenomenon of failing to bring into exist-ence. The vast majority of philosophers who've looked into this don't even believe there *are* such things as nonexistent, possible people, so how could they feel the tragedy—if such it is[12]—of what's-not-there-that-could-possibly-come-into-existence failing to actually come into existence? Note fur-ther that the persons one fails to bring into existence, unlike the victims of murder, are unidentified—indeed, unidentifi-able (by us) —individuals, and it's hard to identify with the unidentifiable. Nevertheless, whether or not it's a tragedy, on my view, there simply are possible persons who fail to make it to existence (and you, the reader, might have been one of them).

Kagan seems to be committing some sort of fal-lacy of large numbers. Consider the case of abortion. If

---

12. Whatever it is, it's probably not *tragedy*, a concept that concerns death, not failing to acquire existence. The fact is, we simply don't have a moral vocabulary with which to assess this phenomenon, which is no less real for that.

abortion really is the killing of innocent persons, the enormous number of abortions performed around the world is a kind of holocaust. Yet pro-choice advocates, presumably, don't sense a holocaust. Pro-life advocates, by contrast, do. As an argument, therefore, against pro-choice advocates, the invocation of *the enormous number* of what they consider innocent persons being killed would be weak. "*If that were true*, a crime of Enormous proportions would be being committed" is never, in itself, a good argument against a set of actions. Imagine trying to dissuade a Nazi by arguing that if Jews really were human beings, the Holocaust being committed would be a crime of Enormous proportions, which, to the Nazi's way of thinking, sounds absurd. I'm reminded of Sarah Silverman's comedy skit: "My niece . . . she called me up and she's like, "Aunt Sarah, did you know Hitler killed 60 million Jews?' I corrected her, and I said, 'You know I think he's responsible for killing *six* million Jews.' And she says, '. . . [S]eriously auntie, what's the difference?' 'The difference is that 60 million Jews is unforgivable, young lady.' Kids. Try to figure them out."

If nonexistence, as such, all else being equal,[13] is bad for us, how much more terrifying is the prospect of nonexistence foreseen, i.e. death. As Kamm puts it: "I strongly suspect that the *terror* of death stems from our awareness of the fact that we will be all over," which she dubs, ominously, "the Extinction Factor."[14] It's easy to fail to appreciate the peculiar mystery, and horror, of nonexistence, since, viewed

13. For example, if it isn't a consequence of acting virtuously.

14. Kamm 1993, 52.

biologically, for living things, death seems "natural,"[15] as does the inevitable destruction of nonliving things. Viewed *ontologically*, however, death and nonexistence are disturbing mysteries, yet all too often it's only at the approach of death that one begins to think ontologically, that one is forced to confront the paradox, and sometimes, terror, of nonexistence. Too late, unfortunately, if one hasn't already learned how to die. Which helps explain why Socrates says in *The Phaedo*: "[T]he one aim of those who practice philosophy in the proper manner is to practice for dying and death" (64a).[16]

In that dialogue, however, Socrates advances arguments that suggest that the soul is immortal. Is that why he believes that those who "practice philosophy in the proper manner" are prepared for death, knowing that death does not, after all, usher in nonexistence? Kagan, apparently, thinks so. "Socrates is actually in a very happy, indeed jovial, mood," he writes, "because [he] thinks that when he dies he is going

15. We are not, however, merely living things; we are persons, with all that that entails. "There is no such thing as a natural death," writes Simone de Beauvoir. "[N]othing that happens to a man is ever natural, since his presence calls the world into question. All men must die: but for every man his death is an accident and, even if he knows it and consents to it, an unjustifiable violation" (*A Very Easy Death*, de Beauvoir 1965, 106). As will soon be seen, however, Socrates doesn't agree with de Beauvoir that every death is an accident or an unjustifiable violation.

16. Learning *how* to die cannot be separated from learning *when* to die. Arthur Droge and James Tabor in *A Noble Death: Suicide and Martyrdom among Christians and Jews in Antiquity* 1992), in discussing the voluntary death of Jews in the assault on Masada, quote from a speech from the Jewish historian Josephus: "Josephus's argument *against* voluntary death in his Jotapata speech is based almost entirely on Plato's discussion in the *Phaedo* of the crucial question: *when ought one to choose death*? He says, 'It is equally cowardly not to wish to die when one *ought to do so*, and to wish to die when one *ought not*'" (94).

to go to a sort of heaven" (2012, 71). To my ears, "jovial," in this context, strikes a discordant note, making it sound as if Socrates's lack of concern about his approaching death is the result of his smug certainty of a cozy afterlife. I think of the use of this term by Charles Dickens in "A Christmas Carol": "For the people who were shoveling away on the house tops were jovial and full of glee; calling out to one another from the parapets, and now and then exchanging a facetious snowball." I don't see Socrates, as his death looms, preparing to exchange a facetious snowball with his disciples.

Interestingly, David Roochnik, in "Play and Seriousness: Plato and Aristotle,"[17] also describes Socrates as "jovial" at the approach of death, but the context in which he applies the term is quite different from the one that frames Kagan's use of the word, since it's precisely not based on the idea that Socrates is smugly certain of a cozy afterlife. According to Roochnik, Plato's doctrines of the immortal soul and the eternal forms are not only not a certainty, they are really "play," albeit, "serious" play, the kind that competitive athletes engage in. Roochnik contrasts this attitude with the self-confident seriousness of Aristotle. In his words, "[O]ne can thus hardly imagine [Aristotle] approaching death with the casual, almost jovial indifference of Socrates in the *Phaedo*." Roochnik, in contrast to Kagan, is, I think, onto something, but I'm still unhappy with his use of the term "jovial" in application to Socrates. Bernard Williams, interestingly, takes the exact opposite tack, speaking instead of "the rather dismal *Phaedo*."[18]

17. Roochnik 2016.

18. *Plato* (Williams 1999, 42).

All three, in my opinion, have it wrong. Socrates is neither jovial nor gloomy as his death approaches. He neither laughs nor cries. His demeanor is pleasant, calm, and reflective. He's not despondent, but neither is he in a mood to party or to throw snowballs. He's in a mood, rather, to philosophize— about death—which he does, up to the last moment. The text of *The Phaedo* may have thrown people off, since it says that "he offered the cup to Socrates who took it quite cheerfully" (117b).[19] "Cheerful," here, as I read it, is not equivalent to "jovial." One should think, rather, of the phrase "be of good cheer," which doesn't mean "be jovial." When the American poet James Russell Lowell wrote, "Let us be of good cheer, however, remembering that the misfortunes hardest to bear are those which never come," he wasn't saying, "Let us be jovial."

Note that *The Phaedo* goes on to say that Socrates took the poison "without tremor or any change of feature or color," i.e. calmly, with equanimity (117b). And a few lines later we're told that Socrates "was holding the cup, and then drained it calmly and easily" (117c). His only irritation came from hearing the commotion caused by his friends' breaking down and weeping, disturbing his peace and tranquility. And the reason for his peace and tranquility, his being "of good cheer," was not, *pace* Kagan, the assurance of a cozy life in the *next* world, but rather his confidence in having lived a virtuous life in *this* world. Gregory Vlastos brings this out forcefully in *Socrates: Ironist and Moral Philosopher*.[20] He refers to what he calls "romanticism," the tendency "[t]o single out

19. *Plato: Five Dialogues*, transl. G. M. A. Grube.

20. Vlastos 1991.

one of the many values in our life, elevating it so far above all the rest that we would choose it at any cost" (233). When in *The Apology* Socrates compares his appointment with death to that of Achilles, what could those two possibly have in common? "Only this," says Vlastos: "absolute subordination of everything each values to one superlatively precious thing: honour for Achilles, virtue for Socrates" (234). Given this, "[W]hat is there to be wondered at," says Vlastos, "if the loss of everything else for virtue's sake leaves you light-hearted, cheerful? . . . [Y]ou hold the secret of your happiness in your own hands. Nothing the world can do can make you unhappy" (235).[21]

As for the question of immortality, from *The Apology* we know that what's striking about Socrates is that when it comes to living a just life, issues concerning the metaphysics of death and the immortality of the soul are irrelevant. "Death," says Socrates, "is something I couldn't care less about . . . [M]y whole concern is not to do anything unjust or impious" (32d). Immortality is a medical, not a moral concept. Socrates does care about his soul, but not because it's immortal. Which is not to say that the soul *isn't* immortal. When Aristotle says in *The Nicomachean Ethics* that the good "will not be good any more for being eternal, since that which lasts long is no whiter than that which perishes in a day" (1096b, in Ackrill 1987), he's quite right. And a virtuous soul will not be any more virtuous if it's eternal. It doesn't follow, however, that a virtuous soul isn't immortal (or that

---

21. Bear in mind that the Greek word *eudaimonia*, usually translated as "happiness," connotes "living well" or "flourishing," whereas, to modern ears, "happiness" puts one in mind of terms like "feeling pleasant," "experiencing joy," or indeed, "being jovial."

the good isn't eternal).[22] What follows is only that if the soul is immortal, its immortality doesn't contribute to its virtue.

Socrates cares about his soul because he believes it's the best part of him, the part ("whatever it is") that's harmed by injustice. And one does not "attend" to one's soul as one "tends" to one's body.[23] One tends to one's body by paying attention to it and its needs. One attends to one's soul by precisely not paying attention to oneself. And that's the point. Socrates, even in *The Apology*, is engaging in metaphysics.[24] He's making, in effect, a type-theoretical or categorial claim: each type or category of entity is (at least partially) defined by its characteristic mode of harm or benefit. You can harm a *performance* of Beethoven's *Moonlight* Sonata if you play the sonata with excessive romanticism, instead of "cleanly," the way Glenn Gould plays it. You can ruin a *score* of the sonata if you spill coffee on it. As for *the sonata itself*, the closest Beethoven could have come to ruining it[25] is if he had messed up some of the harmonies and rhythms. Unlike physical possessions, which are *harmed by destruction*, the

22. Similarly, the number four, an even number, is, for a Platonist, eternal, but it's no more even for being eternal.

23. Or as one "tends" to the Greek gods (by prayer and sacrifice), as Socrates points out in *The Euthyphro*.

24. I can't agree with Vlastos in "Socrates 'contra' Socrates in Plato" (1991, 47) that Socrates$_E$ (the Socrates of the early dialogues) is "exclusively a moral philosopher."

25. I say "the closest he could have come" because it depends on the correct ontology of music. A piece of music that differs at all from the actual *Moonlight* Sonata, as Beethoven wrote it, might not, on some accounts, be that very piece of music. According to this conception, the only way Beethoven could have messed things up would be if he had come close to composing that sonata but instead composed something else.

soul is harmed not by destruction or death but only by *im-morality*[26] (and we ourselves are the only possible authors of that). Being murdered by a Nazi harms your body. Becoming a Nazi harms your soul. For Socrates, as for Simone Weil, it is far worse to cause harm than to suffer it.

That's what's so hard to grasp, and to accept, about Socrates's philosophy, that the value of the soul is independent of the question of immortality.[27] Kamm puts the matter well: "The way in which something ends, rather than simply that it ends, shows us its worth" (1993, 56). One wants to keep *holding onto* things, to grasp them, to possess them. In a sense, Socrates's message is: possession is bad. If you hold "for dear life" onto what you most value, you'll lose it, like a swimmer clutching the lifeguard sent out to save him. As the Bible says, "Whoever loves his life loses it." The chains we forge to bind us to what we hold most dear are simply another kind of prison. "We are drawn towards a thing," writes Simone Weil, "because we believe it is good. We end by being chained to it because it has become necessary."[28] That, I suggest, is part of what Socrates meant when he said in *The Phaedo*, having been released from his chains at the start of

26. Indeed, that's more or less how Socrates defines the soul, as that in us, whatever it is, that's harmed by injustice.

27. I disagree, thus, with Bernard Williams, who writes in "Pagan Justice and Christian Virtue" (2006) that "[t]he sense in which the good man cannot be harmed has to be that he cannot ultimately be harmed. . . . [T]his aspect of Socratic doctrine can make sense only if it is completed, as it was by Plato and by Christianity, with a belief that this is not the only or the most important life we lead . . . that these are [not] the only life and the only friends that we shall ever have. . . . [T]his path leads intelligibly only to . . . a transcendence of finite life altogether" (80).

28. *Gravity and Grace*, 45.

that dialogue (which takes place in a prison), that "the one aim of those who practice philosophy in the proper manner is to practice for dying and death."

Yet those like Gareth Matthews, in "Death in Socrates, Plato, and Aristotle" (2013), who think that Socrates in *The Phaedo* is a different kind of philosopher than Socrates in *The Apology*, fail to see this. "The most I can make of this suggestion myself [about those who practice philosophy in the proper manner]," writes Matthews, "is to take Plato to mean that philosophy is aimed at coming to know the Forms . . . [and that] the soul of the good philosopher will be able to contemplate the Forms eternally" (193). What Socrates is saying, however, in both dialogues, is that if philosophy is done properly, it teaches one how to die,[29] it leads one to contemplate what death means to the good life, whether the soul be mortal or immortal. More particularly, it teaches us that the hope of immortality is not the secret of living a good life.[30] This hard doctrine of Socrates's, early

29. Bertrand Russell wrote—I can't recall the context—words to the effect that if philosophy hasn't prepared you for death, it has failed you. I'm pretty certain he didn't mean that's because "the soul of the good philosopher will be able to contemplate the Forms eternally."

30. Simone Weil was unimpressed by stories of Christian martyrs whose confidence in an afterlife was the source of their courage in the face of death. By contrast, it was precisely Joan of Arc's abjuration from fear of the fire, together with her later reversal, that impressed Weil. "Joan's abjuration," writes Ann Pirruccello, "was [for Weil] evidence of her high spiritual condition. . . . [I]t signifies that she has fully acknowledged the fragility of her life and the possibility that she may cease to exist . . . [For Weil,] Joan was not like the Christian martyrs of legend: she was not convinced of a reward, identified with a supernatural power, or sure of her own immortality so that she could accept death blithely." ("Force or Fragility? Simone Weil and Two Faces of Joan of Arc", 2003, 276).

and late in Plato's dialogues, is, apparently, easy to miss,[31] especially since Socrates himself, in *The Apology*, attempts to soften its edges with playful irony.

Matthews appears to miss the force of both *The Apology* and *The Phaedo*. He recommends, in place of both dialogues, what Aristotle had to say. "Aristotle," he writes, "displays none of the cheerful optimism that radiates from Socrates' last words in the Apology. Nor does he present any of the arguments for the soul's immortality that we find in Plato's Phaedo. Instead, he tries to help us face up to our mortality in a way that will enhance our chances of living worthy lives" (2013, 199). I confess that I can't fathom Matthews's contrasting Socrates (and Plato), on the question of how to face death, with Aristotle. It seems to me that in *The Apology*, precisely what Socrates does is "help us face up to our mortality in a way that will enhance our chances of living worthy

---

31. I can't imagine, however, someone not raising at this point the following objection. "Look, what Socrates himself says at the beginning of *The Phaedo* contradicts what you're saying: 'I should be wrong not to resent dying if I did not believe that I should go first to other wise and good gods, and then to men who have died and are better than men are here' (63c)." Socrates does indeed say this, but note that earlier, he remarked that he's spent his time in jail putting Aesop's tales into verse. Is he not, in the quoted passage, spinning more fairy tales to calm the nerves of his disciples (as Plato is, of his readers), who are no doubt among those he speaks of later who are scared of death, as children are of the dark? Recall that at the close of *The Apology*, he also spins a fairy tale, musing that "[i]f . . . death is a change from here to another place, and what we are told is true and all who have died are there, what greater blessing could there be" (40 e), although it's quite clear he doesn't really know what happens when you die, and that that has no effect on his being willing to die if justice demands it. It should come as no surprise to be told that both Socrates and Plato mix fairy tales in with their philosophy, and that the philosophers among us are expected to be able to distinguish the two.

lives," by insisting that death is of no concern to the virtuous. And to speak of Socrates's "cheerful optimism" is misleading in the extreme, since nothing could be harder, more difficult to accept, than the doctrine of virtue espoused by Socrates according to which concern for death—and perhaps permanent oblivion—is strikingly absent:

"Socrates, I don't want to die. The last ten soldiers who took on the Spartans were slaughtered. You've got to tell me: is there hope of life after death?"

"Be quiet, man! Death is something I couldn't care less about. You know your duty. Now go and do it!"[32]

"Thanks, Socrates. I really appreciate your cheerful optimism."

As for Aristotle "not presenting any of the arguments for the soul's immortality that we find in Plato's Phaedo," has Matthews forgotten the famous (and mysterious) ending of Aristotle's *De Anima*, in which he says of the "active intellect" that "this intellect is distinct, unaffected, and unmixed, being in essence activity," and that "[i]n separation it is just what it is, and this alone is immortal and eternal"? (430a15, in Ackrill 1987).

And concerning Socrates's "suggestions" in *The Apology* about what might happen after death, should it not have been obvious that he was being playful when he imagined that perhaps the afterlife will offer us not a place where one

32. Cf. *Apology* 32d: "[D]eath is something I couldn't care less about" (Grube translation), and *Apology* 28b: "Man, you don't speak well if you believe that someone worth anything at all would give countervailing weight to danger of life or death or give consideration to anything but this when he acts: whether his action is just or unjust" (translation from Vlastos 1991, 233).

meets one's maker and "all secrets are revealed," but rather an opportunity to do more philosophizing? As if heaven were not a place where we find God, but rather a place where we can continue the search for God. Or that Socrates was being playful when he mused that perhaps at death we'll simply fall into a relaxing and wonderful, dreamless sleep, reminiscent of the most pleasant nights we spent during our lives. Dreamlessness, of course, is crucial. Hamlet, contemplating suicide, agrees: "To sleep, perchance to dream—ay, there's the rub. For in that sleep of death what dreams may come." It should be obvious, however, that this is not a rare case of Socrates, in a serious mood, waxing metaphysical about the afterlife. Are we really to believe that he's forgotten that the reason we enjoy a good night's sleep is that we *wake up* refreshed in the morning? Matthews, apparently, believes the answer is yes, affirming, flatfootedly, that "Socrates thinks that if death is eternal oblivion, it may be like the blessings of a dreamless sleep" (2013, 193),

To be sure, by contrast with Socrates in *The Apology*, Socrates in *The Phaedo* is concerned to discover the truth about the immortality of the soul and the ontology of death, but it's still *Socrates*. When he said in *The Apology* that "death is something I couldn't care less about," he was focusing his attention on the good life and emphasizing the fact that it's not founded on the correct ontology of death. The soldier who falls on a grenade to save his comrades is not relying on his belief in an afterlife. He simply knows what's the right thing to do, and does it. There's no reason to believe, however, that Socrates even in *The Apology* had no interest in discovering what kind of being he is . He affirms, after all, that your soul is *the kind of thing* that is harmed by committing injustice. What could be more natural than proceeding to inquire *what kind of thing* that is? Matthews and Kagan, however, are mistaken in assuming that since Socrates in *The Phaedo* considers the possibility that the soul is immortal, that's *the reason* he faces his death with equanimity.

Recall, moreover, that when Simmias confesses to "some private misgivings" about the final argument for the immortality of the soul, Socrates says this is the right thing to say, adding that "our first hypotheses require closer examination." (107b) There's no knockout in this fight, only a series of body blows to the prejudice that we know just what we are.[33] The old Socratic virtue is firmly in place: not believing we know what we don't know. At the same time, there's no reason to doubt that it remains true that for Socrates—and Plato—our ultimate harm comes from our own injustice, and thus a just life, a philosophical life, is the ultimate good. If, in the end, it turns out that none of the arguments for the immortality of the soul in *The Phaedo* prove convincing, and no others can be found that are more compelling, we will have to accept the fact that we emerged from nonexistence and will return to it. Death will then serve as an invitation to us, the living, to grasp our true nature as travelers from nonexistence to existence, and back again. Is it not a good thing to discover what we are? "Or don't you suppose," as Socrates says in *Charmides*,[34] "that it is a common good for almost all human beings that each thing that exists should become

---

33. As Gödel said: "We do not know *what* we are (namely in essence and seen eternally)" (quoted in Wang 1987, 215).

34. Plato (1986), 166d.

clearly apparent just as it is?" Will this not change our lives? "[For Plato,] one will find one's life changed," wrote Bernard Williams, "through . . . dialectical discussion of such things as the metaphysical problems of not being,"[35] metaphysical problems that help reveal the nature of the beings we are.

35. Williams (1999), 44.

BIBLIOGRAPHY

Ackrill, J. L., ed. 1987. *A New Aristotle Reader*. Princeton, NJ: Princeton University Press.

Adams, R. 1989. "Time and Thisness." In Almog, Perry, and Wettstein 1989, 23–42.

Albert, D. and Galchen, R. 2009. "Was Einstein Wrong? A Quantum Threat to Special Relativity." *Scientific American Magazine*. https://www.scientificamerican.com/article/was-einstein-wrong-about-relativity/.

Almog, J., Perry, J., and Wettstein, H., eds. 1989. *Themes from Kaplan*. New York: Oxford University Press.

Anderson, C. A. 1990. "Some Emendations of Gödel's Ontological Proof." *Faith and Philosophy* 7 (3): 291–303.

Anderson, C. A. and Gettings, M. 1996. "Gödel's Ontological Proof Revisited." In P. Hájek, ed., *Gödel '96: Logical Foundatons of Mathematics, Computer Science and Physics—Kurt Gödel's Legacy*. Berlin: Springer, 167–172.

van Atten, M. 2004. *On Brouwer*. Canada: Thomson Wadsworth.

van Atten, M. 2007. *Brouwer Meets Husserl: On the Phenomenology of Choice Sequences*. Dordrecht, The Netherlands: Springer

Barwise, J. and Perry, J. 1981. "Semantic Innocence and Uncompromising Situations." In P. French, T. Uehling Jr., and H. Wettstein, eds., *Midwest Studies in Philosophy*, vol. 6. Minneapolis: University of Minnesota Press, 387–404.

Barwise, J. and Perry, J. 1983. *Situations and Attitudes*. Cambridge, MA: MIT Press.

Beaney, M., ed. 1997. *The Frege Reader*. Oxford: Blackwell.

de Beauvoir, S. 1965. *A Very Easy Death*. Transl P. O'Brian. New York: Pantheon Books.

Bell, J. S. 1989. "How to Teach Special Relativity." In *Speakable and Unspeakable in Quantum Mechanics*. Cambridge: Cambridge University Press, 67–80.

Benardete, J. 1989. *Metaphysics: The Logical Approach*. Oxford: Oxford University Press.

Bernstein, J. 1991. *Quantum Profiles*. Princeton: Princeton University Press.

Bourne, C. 2006. *A Future for Presentism*. Oxford: Clarendon Press.

Bradley, B., Feldman, F., and Johansson, J., eds. 2013. *The Oxford Handbook of Philosophy of Death*. Oxford: Oxford University Press.

Brumfiel, G. 2001. "How Raindrops Form." *Physical Review Focus* 7, 14. https://physics.aps.org/story/v7/st14.

Burgess, J. P. 2013. *Saul Kripke: Puzzles and Mysteries*. Cambridge, UK: Polity Press.

Čapek, M. 1961. *The Philosophical Impact of Contemporary Physics*. New York: Van Nostrand.

Čapek, M., ed. 1976. *The Concepts of Space and Time*. Dordrecht: Reidel.

Carnap, R. 1963. "Intellectual Autobiography." In P. A. Schilpp, ed., *The Philosophy of Rudolph Carnap*. La Salle: Open Court, 37–63.

Chargaff, E. 1986. "Swindle—Scientific and Otherwise." In *Serious Questions: An ABC of Skeptical Reflections*. Boston: Birkhäuser, 193–205.

Cornford, F. M., transl. *Plato and Parmenides: Parmenides' Way of Truth and Plato's Parmenides*. New York: Liberal Arts Press, 1957.

Connolly, N. 2011. "How the Dead Live." *Philosophia* 39 (1), 83–103.

Dilworth, T. 1995. "Cummings' 'Buffalo Bill's.'" *Explicator* 53 (3), 174–75.

Donnellan, K. 1974. "Speaking of Nothing." *Philosophical Review* 83 (1), 3–31.

Donnellan, K. 2012. *Essays on Reference, Language, and Mind.* Oxford: Oxford Unversity Press.

Droge, A. J. and Tabor, J. D. 1992. *A Noble Death: Suicide and Martyrdom among Christians and Jews in Antiquity.* HarperSanFrancisco.

Dummett, M. 1978. *Elements of Intuitionism.* Oxford: Clarendon Press.

Einstein, A. 1961. *Relativity: The Special and General Theory.* New York: Crown Publishers.

Einstein, A. 1976. "Comments on Meyerson's *La Deduction Relativiste.*" In Čapek 1976, 363–67.

Ellis, G. F. R. 1996. "Contributions of K. Gödel to Relativity and Cosmology." In Hájek, 1969, 34–49.

Esfeld, M. 2015. "Quantum Physics and Presentism." In A. von Müller, ed., *Re-thinking Time at the Interface of Physics and Philosophy: The Forgotten Present.* Berlin: Springer.

Feldman, R. 1992. *Confrontations with the Reaper: A Philosophical Study of the Nature and Value of Death.* New York: Oxford University Press.

Fine, K. 2005. *Modality and Tense: Philosophical Papers.* Oxford: Clarendon Press.

Fischer, J. M., ed. 1993. *The Metaphysics of Death.* Stanford, CA: Stanford University Press.

Frege, G. 1980. *The Foundations of Arithmetic: A Logico-Mathematical Enquiry into the Concept of Number.* Transl. J. L. Austin. Evanston, IL: Northwestern University Press.

French, P. and Wettstein, H., eds. 2000. *Life and Death: Metaphysics and Ethics.* Midwest Studies in Philosophy, vol. 24. Hoboken, NJ: Wiley-Blackwell.

Furth, M. 1974. "Elements of Eleatic Ontology." In A. P. D. Mourelatos, ed., *The Pre-Socratics: A Collection of Critical Essays.* Garden City, NY: Anchor Books, 241–70.

Furth, M. 1988. *Substance, Form and Psyche: An Aristotelian Metaphysics.* Cambridge: Cambridge University Press.

García-Carpintero, M. and Martí, G., eds. 2014. *Empty Representations: Reference and Non-existence.* Oxford: Oxford University Press.

Geach, P. 1969. *God and the Soul.* Bristol: Thoemmes Press.

Gilson, E. 1952. *Being and Some Philosophers*. Toronto: Pontifical Institute of Mediaeval Studies.

Gödel, K. 1990. "A Remark about the Relationship between Relativity Theory and Idealistic Philosophy." In Yourgrau 1990, 261–65.

Hájek, P. ed. 1996. *Gödel '96: Logical Foundations of Mathematics, Computer Science and Physics – Kurt Gödel's Legacy*. Berlin Heidelberg: Springer-Verlag.

Hallet, M. 1984. *Cantorian Set Theory and Limitation of Size*. Oxford: Clarendon Press.

Hawking, S., and Ellis, G.F. R. 1973. *The Large Scale Structure of Space-Time*. New York, New York: Cambridge University Press.

Heisenberg, W. 1962. *Physics and Philosophy: The Revolution in Modern Science*. New York: Harper & Row.

Heyd, D. 1994. *Genethics: Moral Issues in the Creation of People*. Berkeley: University of California Press.

Hinchliff, M. 2000. "A Defense of Presentism in a Relativistic Setting." *Philosophy of Science* 67, S575–S586.

Hintikka, J. 1986. "Kant on Existence, Predication, and the Ontological Argument." In S. Knuuttila and J. Hintikka, eds., *The Logic of Being: Historical Studies*. Dordrecht: D. Reidel, 249–67.

Hirsch, E. 1982. *The Concept of Identity*. New York: Oxford University Press.

Horwich, P. 1990. "The Growth of Now." Review of J. R. Lucas, *The Future*. *Times Literary Supplement*, 672.

Hossack, K. 2007. *The Metaphysics of Knowledge*. Oxford: Oxford University Press.

Hughes, C. 2004. *Kripke: Names, Necessity, Identity*. Oxford: Clarendon Press.

Isaacson, W. 2007. *Einstein: His Life and Universe*. New York: Simon & Schuster.

Isaacson, W. 2017. *Leonardo da Vinci*. New York: Simone & Schuster.

Ishiguro, H. 1980. "Possibility." *Proceedings of the Aristotelian Society*, suppl. vol. 44, 73–87.

Jeffrey, R. 1980. "Coming True." In C. Diamond and J. Teichman, eds., *Intention and Intentionality*. Ithaca, NY: Cornell University Press, 251–60.

Kagan, S. 2012. *Death*. New Haven: Yale University Press.

Kamm, F. 1993. *Morality, Mortality*. Vol. 1, *Death and Whom to Save from It*. New York: Oxford University Press.

Kant, I. 1965. *Critique of Pure Reason*. Transl. N. K. Smith. New York: St. Martin's Press.

Kaplan, D. 1970. "What Is Russell's Theory of Descriptions?" In W. Yourgrau and A. D. Breck, eds., *Physics, Logic and History*. New York: Plenum Press, 277–95.

Kaplan, D. 1973. "Bob and Carol and Ted and Alice." In J. Hintikka, J. M. E. Moravcsik, and P. Suppes, eds., *Approaches to Natural Language*. Dordrecht: D. Reidel, 490–518.

Kaplan, D. 1979. "Transworld Heir Lines." In M. J. Loux, ed., *The Possible and the Actual: Readings in the Metaphysics of Modality*. Ithaca: Cornell University Press, 88–109.

Kaplan, D. 1989a. "Demonstratives." In Almog, Perry, and Wettstein 1989, 481–563.

Kaplan, D. 1989b. "Afterthoughts." In Almog, Perry, and Wettstein 1989, 565–614.

Kaplan, D. 2005. "Reading 'On Denoting' on Its Centenary." *Mind* 114 (456), 933–1000.

Kieran, M. 2005. *Revealing Art*. New York: Routledge.

Kneale, W. 1936. "Is Existence a Predicate?" *Proceedings of the Aristotelian Society*, suppl. vol. 15, 29–43.

Kripke, S. 1971. "Semantical Considerations on Modal Logic." In L. Linsky, ed., *Reference and Modality*. Oxford: Oxford University Press, 63–72.

Kripke, S. 1974a. "First General Discussion Session." *Synthese* 27, 471–508.

Kripke, S. 1974b. "Second General Discussion Session." *Synthese* 27, 509–21.

Kripke, S. 1977. "Is There a Problem about Substitutional Quantification?" In G. Evans and J. McDowell, eds., *Truth and Meaning: Essays in Semantics*. Oxford: Clarendon Press, 325–419.

Kripke, S. 1980. *Naming and Necessity*. Cambridge, MA: Harvard University Press.

Kripke, S. 1993. "Identity and Necessity." In A.W. Moore, ed., *Meaning and Reference*. Oxford: Oxford University Press, 162–91.

Kripke, S. 2005. "Russell's Notion of Scope." *Mind* 114 (456), 1005–37.

Kripke, S. 2011. "The First Person." In S. Kripke, *Philosophical Troubles: Collected Papers Volume 1*. Oxford: Oxford Univesity Press, 292–321.

Kripke, S. 2013. *Reference and Existence: The John Locke Lectures*. New York: Oxford University Press.

Lewis, D. 1986. *On the Plurality of Worlds*. Oxford: Basil Blackwell Ltd.

Luper, S. 2009. *The Philosophy of Death*. Cambridge: Cambridge University Press.

Luper, S., ed. 2014a. *The Cambridge Companion to Life and Death*. Cambridge: Cambridge University Press.

Luper, S. 2014b. "Death." *Stanford Encyclopedia of Philosophy*, Winter 2014 ed.

Luper, S. 2018. "Never Existing." *Mortality: Promoting the Interdisciplinary Study of Death and Dying* 23 (2), 173–83.

Luper, S. No date. "Nonexistence." Draft.

Marcus, R. B. 1993. "Possibilia and Possible Worlds." In *Modalities: Philosophical Essays*. New York: Oxford University Press, 189–213.

Matthews, G. B. 2013. "Death in Socrates, Plato, and Aristotle." In Bradley, Feldman, and Johansson 2013, 186–99.

Maudlin, T. 1994. *Quantum Non-locality and Relativity*. Oxford: Basil Blackwell.

Maudlin, T. 2001. "Remarks on the Passing of Time." *Proceedings of the Aristotelian Society* 102 (3), 237–52.

Maudlin, T. 2007. "On the Passing of Time." In T. Maudlin, *The Metaphysics within Physics*. Oxford: Oxford University Press, 104–42.

Maudlin, T. 2014. *New Foundations for Physical Geometry: The Theory of Linear Structures*. Oxford: Oxford University Press.

Maudlin, T. 2017. "A Defense of the Reality of Time." *Quanta Magazine*. https://www.quantamagazine.org/a-defense-of-the-reality-of-time-20170516/.

Mellor, D. H. 1981. *Real Time*. Cambridge: Cambridge University Press.

Menzel, C. 2014. "Classical Possibilism and Lewisian Possibilism." Supplement to "Actualism." *Stanford Encyclopedia of Philosophy*.

Summer 2014 ed. https://plato.stanford.edu/entries/actualism/possibilism.html.

Moore, G. E. 1978. *Some Main Problems of Philosophy*. London: George Allen & Unwin LTD.

Mozersky, M. J. 2015. *Time, Language, and Ontology: The World from the B-Theoretic Perspective*. Oxford: Oxford University Press.

Nagel, T. 1986. *The View from Nowhere*. Oxford: Oxford University Press.

Nagel, T. 1993. "Death." In Fischer 1993, 61–69.

Ockham, W. 1983. *Predestination, God's Foreknowledge, and Future Contingents*. Transl. M. M. Adams and N. Kretzmann. Indianapolis: Hackett.

Parfit, D. 2011. "On What There Is." Appendix J in *On What Matters*, vol. 2. Oxford: Oxford University Press, 719–49.

Parfit, D. 2017. "Future People, the Non-identity Problem, and Person-Affecting Principles." *Philosophy and Public Affairs* 45 (2), 118–57.

Parsons, C. 1982. "Objects and Logic." *The Monist* 65, 491–516.

Parsons, C. 1983. *Mathematics in Philosophy: Selected Essays*. Ithaca, NY: Cornell University Press.

Parsons, C. 2008. *Mathematical Thought and Its Objects*. Cambridge: Cambridge University Press.

Parsons, C. 2010. "Gödel and Philosophical Idealism." *Philosophia Mathematica* 18, 166–92.

Pirruccello, A. (2003). "Force or Fragility? Simone Weil and Two Faces of Joan of Arc." In A. W. Astell and B. Wheeller, eds., *Joan of Arc and Spirituality*. New York, Palgrave Macmillan, 267 – 81.

Plantinga, A. 1978. *The Nature of Necessity*. Oxford: Clarendon Press.

Plantinga, A. 2007. "On Existentialism." In M. Davidson, ed., *On Sense and Direct Reference*. Boston: McGraw Hill, 544–68.

Plato. 1986. *Charmides*. Transl. T. G. West and G. S. West. Indianapolis: Hackett.

Plato. 2002. Transl. G. M. A. Grube. Revised by John M. Cooper. *Plato: Five Dialogues*. Indianapolis: Hackett.

Popper, K. 1965. "Of Clouds and Clocks: An Approach to the Problem of Rationality and the Freedom of Man." The Arthur Holly Compton Memorial Lecture Presented at Washington University, April 21, 1965. St. Louis, Missouri: Washington University, 1–38.

Popper, K. 1982. *The Open Universe: An Argument for Indeterminism.* Totowa, NJ: Rowman and Littlefield.

Popper, K. 1984. "A Critical Note on the Greatest Days of Quantum Mechanics." In A. O. Barut, A. van der Merwe, and J.-P. Vigier, eds., *Quantum, Space, and Time: The Quest Continues. Studies and Essays in Honour of Louis de Broglie, Paul Dirac and Eugene Wigner.* Cambridge: Cambridge University Press, 49–54.

Priest, G. 2003. "Meinongianism and the Philosophy of Mathematics." *Philosophia Mathematica* 11, 3–15.

Prior, A. 2010. "Identifiable Individuals." In *Papers on Time and Tense,* ed. P. Hasle, P. Ohrstrom, T. Brauner, and J. Copeland. Oxford: Oxford University Press, 81–92.

Putnam, H. 1979. "Time and Physical Geometry." In *Mathematics, Matter, and Method: Philosophical Papers,* Vol. 1. Cambridge: Cambridge University Press, 198–205.

Quine, W. V. O. 1961. "On What There Is." In *From a Logical Point of View.* New York: Harper & Row, 1–19.

Quine, W. V. O. 1969. "Existence and Quantification." In *Ontological Relativity and Other Essays.* New York: Columbia University Press, 91–113.

Quine, W. V. O. 1979. "Quantifiers and Propositional Attitudes." In *The Ways of Paradox and Other Essays.* Cambridge, MA: Harvard University Press, 185–96.

Quine, W. V. O. 1987. *Quiddities: An Intermittently Philosophical Dictionary.* Cambridge, MA: Belknap Press of Harvard University Press.

Rescher, N. 2003. *Imagining Irreality: A Study of Unreal Possibilities.* Chicago: Open Court.

Roochnik, D. 2016. "Play and Seriousness: Plato and Aristotle." *Spaziofilosofico* 18, 439–51. http://www.spaziofilosofico.it/tag/david-roochnik/.

Russell, B. 1903. *The Principles of Mathematics.* New York: Norton.

Russell, B. 1905. "On Denoting." *Mind* 14 (56), 479–93.

Sainsbury, R. M. 2010. *Fiction and Fictionalism.* New York: Routledge.

Salmon, N. 2008a. *Metaphysics, Mathematics, and Meaning.* Oxford: Clarendon Press.

Salmon, N. 2008b. "Existence." In Salmon 2008a, 9–49.

Salmon, N. 2008c. "Nonexistence." In Salmon 2008a, 50–90.

Salmon, N. 2008d. "An Empire of Thin Air." In Salmon 2008a, 122–28.

Salmon, N. 2014. "What Is Existence?" In García-Carpintero and Martí 2014, 245–61.

Salmon, N. and Soames, S., eds. 1988. *Propositions and Attitudes.* Oxford: Oxford University Press.

Saunders, S. 2002. "How Relativity Contradicts Presentism." In C. Callender, ed., *Time, Reality, and Experience.* Cambridge: Cambridge University Press, 277–92.

Scanlon, T. 2000. *What We Owe To Each Other.* Cambridge, MA: Belknap Press.

Scholem, G. 1995. *Major Trends in Jewish Mysticism.* New York: Schocken Books.

Sharvy, R. 1968. "Why a Class Can't Change Its Members." *Noûs* 2, 303–14.

Sharvy, R. 1969. "Things." *The Monist* 53, 488–504.

Shimony, A. 1993. "The Transient Now." In A. Shimony, *Search for a Naturalistic World View,* Vol. II. Cambridge: Cambridge University Press, 271–87.

Sider, T. 2003. *Four-Dimensionalism: An Ontology of Persistence and Time.* Oxford: Clarendon Press.

Sider, T. 2013. "The Evil of Death: What Can Metaphysics Contribute?" In Bradley, Feldman, and Johansson 2013, 155–66.

Sigmund, K. 2017. *Exact Thinking in Demented Times: The Vienna Circle and the Epic Quest for the Foundations of Science.* New York: Basic Books.

Silverstein, H. 1993. "The Evil of Death." In Fischer 1993, 95–116.

Silverstein, H. 2000. "The Evil of Death Revisited." In French and Wettstein 2000, 116–34.

Skow, B. 2015. *Objective Becoming.* Oxford: Oxford University Press.

Sobel, J. H. 1987. "Gödel's Ontological Proof." In J. J. Thomson, ed., *On Being and Saying: Essays for Richard Cartwright.* Cambridge, MA: MIT Press, 241–61.

von Solodkov, T. 2014. "Fictional Realism and Negative Existentials." In García-Carpintero and Martí 2014, 333–52.

Solomyak, O. 2013. "Actuality and the Amodal Perspective." *Philosophical Studies* 164 (1), 15–40.

Stachel, J. 2007. Review of *A World without Time: The Forgotten Legacy of Gödel and Einstein*. *Notices of the American Mathematical Society* 54 (7), 861–68.

Stalnaker, R. 1979. "Possible Worlds." In M. J. Loux, ed., *The Possible and the Actual*. Ithaca, NY: Cornell University Press, 225–34.

Stein, H. 1968. "On Einstein-Minkowski Space-Time." *The Journal of Philosophy*, 65, 5–23.

Strawson, P. F. 1950. "On Referring." *Mind* 259 (235), 320–44.

Strawson, P. F. 1963. *Individuals: An Essay in Descriptive Metaphysics*. Garden City, NY: Anchor Books.

Strawson, P. F. 1974. "Aesthetic Appraisal and Works of Art." In *Freedom and Resentment and Other Essays*. London: Methuen, 178–88.

Tieszen, R. 2011. *After Gödel: Platonism and Rationalism in Mathematics and Logic*. Oxford: Oxford University Press.

Thomason, R. 1970. "Indeterminist Time and Truth-Value Gaps." *Theoria*, XXXVI, 264–81.

Thomson, J. J. 1971. "A Defense of Abortion." *Philosophy and Public Affairs* 1 (1), 47–66.

Thomson, J. J. 1997. "People and Their Bodies." In J. Dancy, ed., *Reading Parfit*. Oxford: Blackwell, 202 – 29.

Van Inwagen, P. 1990. *Material Beings*. Ithaca, NY: Cornell University Press.

Van Inwagen, P. 2014. "Being, Existence, and the Ontological Argument." In *Existence: Essays in Ontology*. Cambridge: Cambridge University Press, 50–115.

Vlastos, G. 1981. *Platonic Studies*. 2nd printing with corrections. Princeton, NJ: Princeton University Press.

Vlastos, G. 1991. *Socrates: Ironist and Moral Philosopher*. Ithaca, NY: Cornell University Press.

Wang, H. 1974. *From Mathematics to Philosophy*. London: Routledge.

Wang, H. 1987. *Reflections on Kurt Gödel*. Cambridge, MA: MIT Press.

Wang, H. 1996. *A Logical Journey: From Gödel to Philosophy*. Cambridge, MA: MIT Press.

Weil, S. 1992. *Gravity and Grace*. Transl. E. Craufurd. London: Routledge.

Wetzel, L. 2000. "Is Socrates Essentially a Man?" *Philosophical Studies* 98, 203–20.

Wiljdeveld, P. 2000. *Ludwig Wittgenstein: Architect.* Amsterdam: Pepin Press.

Williams, B. 1999. *Plato.* New York: Routledge.

Williams, B. 2006. *The Sense of the Past: Essays in the History of Philosophy.* Ed. M. Burnyeat. Princeton, NJ: Princeton University Press.

Williamson, T. 2002. "Nonexistents." In A. O'Hear, ed., *Logic, Thought, and Language.* Cambridge: Cambridge University Press, 233–51.

Williamson, T. 2013. *Modal Logic as Metaphysics.* Oxford: Oxford University Press.

Wittgenstein, L. 1961. *Tractatus Logico-Philosophicus.* Transl. D. R. Pears and B. F. McGuinness. London: Routledge & Kegan Paul.

Wolchover, N. 2016. "Quantum Gravity's Time Problem." *Quantamagazine.* https://www.quantamagazine.org/20161201-quantum-gravitys-time-problem/.

Wright, C. 1983. *Frege's Conception of Numbers as Objects.* Aberdeen: Aberdeen University Press.

Wüthrich, C. 2013. "The Fate of Presentism in Modern Physics." In R. Ciunti, K. Miller, and G. Torrengo, eds., *New Papers on the Present: Focus on Presentism.* Munich: Philosophia Verlag.

Yourgrau, P. 1982. "Frege, Perry, and Demonstratives." *Canadian Journal of Philosophy* 12, 725–52.

Yourgrau, P. 1985. "Russell and Kaplan on Denoting." *Philosophy and Phenomenological Research* 46, 315–21.

Yourgrau, P. 1986. "On Time and Actuality: The Dilemma of Privileged Possession." *British Journal for the Philosophy of Science* 37, 405–17.

Yourgrau, P. 1987. "Frege on Truth and Reference." *Notre Dame Journal of Formal Logic* 28, 132–38.

Yourgrau, P., ed. 1990a. *Demonstratives.* Oxford: Oxford University Press.

Yourgrau, P. 1990b "The Path Back to Frege." In Yourgrau, 1990a, 97–132.

Yourgrau, P. 1993. "The Dead." In Fischer 1993, 137–56.

Yourgrau, P. 1999. *Gödel Meets Einstein: Time Travel in the Gödel Universe.* Chicago: Open Court.

Yourgrau, P. 2000. "Can the Dead Really Be Buried?" In French and Wettstein 2000, 46–68.

Yourgrau, P. 2006. *A World without Time: The Forgotten Legacy of Gödel and Einstein*. New York: Basic Books.

Yourgrau, P. 2007. Letter to the Editor: "Review of *A World without Time*." *Notices of the American Mathematical Society* 54 (10), 1281.

Yourgrau, P. 2011. *Simone Weil*. London: Reaktion Books.

Yourgrau, P. 2012. "Kripke's Frege." *Thought* 1, 100–107.

Yourgrau, P. 2013. "Kripke's Moses." In J. S. Taylor, ed., *The Metaphysics and Ethics of Death: New Essays*. Oxford: Oxford University Press, 134–48.

Yourgrau, P. 2014. "When Time Turned into Space." *Spaziofilosofico* 11, 205–12.

Yourgrau, P. 2015. "On Time and Intuitionism." An invited talk before the Clavius Group of Catholic Mathematicians at the College of the Holy Cross on July 7, 2015.

INDEX